**Early Childhood
Intervention
and Juvenile
Delinquency**

Early Childhood Intervention and Juvenile Delinquency

Edited by
Fernand N. Dutile
University of Notre Dame
Cleon H. Foust
Indiana Lawyers Commission
D. Robert Webster
Senior Attorney,
    Cummins Engine Company

LexingtonBooks
D.C. Heath and Company
Lexington, Massachusetts
Toronto

Library of Congress Cataloging in Publication Data

Main entry under title:
  Early childhood intervention and juvenile delinquency.

  "Product of the Juvenile Delinquency and Early Childhood Intervention
Conference held in Indianapolis, Indiana on May 7, 8, and 9, 1981"—Pref.
  1. Juvenile delinquency—United States—Congresses. 2. Juvenile
delinquency—United States—Prevention—Congresses. 3. Child development—
United States—Congresses. I. Dutile, Fernand N. II. Foust, Cleon H.
III. Webster, D. Robert. IV. Juvenile Delinquency and Early Childhood
Intervention Conference (1981: Indianapolis, Ind.)
HV9104.E25   364.3'6'0973   81-47973
ISBN 0-669-05204-3   AACR2

Published simultaneously in Canada

Printed in the United States of America

International Standard Book Number: 0-669-05204-3

Library of Congress Catalog Card Number: 81-47973

To my children, Dan and Patty Dutile
                                    F.N.D.

To my mother, Lela Grace Foust
                                    C.H.F.

*To my mother and father, Afra L. and
     Dolphus F. Webster*
                                    D.R.W.

Contents

Foreword

Unlike Congress, state legislatures, or governors, a foundation does not have yardsticks or competitors or even last year's sales figures or earnings per share to evaluate its performance and guide its objectives. It faces no deadlines, and it need not achieve measurable success in a two-year or four-year period. Most problems are not solved, sometimes not even analyzed, in a biennium or a four-year term. The problems this book addresses are in that frustrating group not solved by biennial budgets, special regulations, or executive edicts. We who have been in Indiana government and foundation work know how long it takes to accomplish anything worthwhile in the field of criminal justice.

But thanks in large part to the Indiana Lawyers Commission, we have made major progress in these eight years in Indiana; we are no longer close to the bottom. We do have new criminal, juvenile, and corrections codes and other programs as well.

We all long for simple answers to complex personal problems. The same is true for social ills, particularly for crime. I believe people do not want to think about crime but merely to emote about it. How do we determine whether what we have been prescribing for crime brings value received? Take ten years of confinement at $100,000; is it better or worse than the lash or the ducking stool or the punishments in Saudi Arabia? What did we really expect to achieve through the Law Enforcement Assistance Administration? How much crime is a community willing to tolerate?

How much is a state willing to pay to reduce crime? Criminal-justice expenditures—particularly those for corrections—are almost always near the bottom of legislative budgetary priorities. Money spent for criminal justice is in reality defense spending, and if it actually produces little defense it is analogous to buying five million bows and a billion arrows to deter military threats from the Soviet Union. The real truth is we do not know how effective our crime defense is; reports are conflicting. The one thing we do know is that we spend literally billions, and crime increases.

Each year we learn more about the range of our ignorance. We do not know, for example, how much prevention and deterrence to crime we are buying. We do not know what effect long imprisonment has on the crime rate (probably some, but we tend to forget that sooner or later that violent person will be freed). We do not know how to predict violence or how to handle it if we could predict it. We do not know what rehabilitates. We only know that we are not getting the job done.

Purposely, I have stated a rather bleak picture without much exaggeration. I have taken this approach to emphasize that we are not really getting anywhere with an emotional approach to crime. We must *think* about crime for a change.

The objectives of this book include trying to find out things we do not know about early intervention. We do know that in a free society we cannot eliminate the risk of crime, but then what are *acceptable* risks? We judge some risks calmly everyday—for example, walking against the light at a busy intersection, increasing the deductible on our house-theft policy, taking more than two social drinks or 3,000 calories of food daily, checking ten years certain as an option on a pension plan, or assuming smog, air-pollutant health risks that accompany city living.

Another "strange" risk relevant to the topic of this book is that we treat junior-high youngsters from 8 A.M. to 4 P.M. as they were irresponsible children, but from 4 P.M. to midnight we give them, as baby sitters, total responsibility for the well-being of our children and grandchildren and expect them to act like adults (preferably *better* than adults).

Consider the risks we take at day-care centers: We drop off our children and place them for most of their waking hours with (usually) untrained, underpaid people who, nevertheless, *care*.

What specific risks have we taken in the way we treat status offenders? Is their population in public and private juvenile facilities declining? And, if so, for the wrong reasons? To what risks do we expose our children with present child-labor laws, and how could those risks evolve with thoughtful changes in those laws? Whom do those laws really protect? Do they help build self-respect?

Should there be a research project done among migrant families in order to secure a sophisticated analysis of people of all ages needing people of all ages? Or is there an innate or gradually developing basic understanding of people of all ages needing people of all ages as well as a strong sense of mutual need and mutual worth?

How much crime is caused by a bad self-image? By bad example? By idleness? How old must a child be to want to be an individual? To be treated with respect? At what age and in what way is basic self-respect—not ego-building or egocentric self-respect—determined? At what point can one detect the child who lacks that basic self-respect? Who has that bad self-image? When and how do we know what he lacks? And who decides?

Are we willing to admit that almost everyone can be more objective about someone else's children and grandchildren? What can we learn from cottage industries and migrant families and communal living? How do we examine our need for each other and recognize how natural it is to take the best from each other? Do we need an advanced degree to analyze that concept, or can we just practice and feel and live with certain risks—whatever we determine they are?

There are even risks in statistics. Forty percent of foster parents remain foster parents for less than a year; only six states have compulsory training for foster parents; some judges callously refer to public costs as the "hay, oats, and water" questions of juvenile delinquency. It now costs an average of $12,000 a year to maintain a child in a public correctional facility.

Consider another thought. The first penitentiary in this country was built by the Quakers in Philadelphia as a rehabilitation technique. As such, it has not been successful and now, years later, as a prison, it has become the dominating factor in our whole criminal structure. We put more people per capita in it than any country in the Western world except South Africa. Few people would favor wholly abolishing prisons; we must tolerate prisons for the violent and incorrigible. But must prisons *dominate* our criminal-justice system? What further public consideration is needed?

Applying some original thought to the problem of crime could lead to new approaches and cost-effective analyses that would pay off in a reduction of offenses. In a sense, that is what this book aims for: not only to discuss early childhood intervention but to formulate new techniques and strategies to foreclose developing criminality. Let us examine what risks we have the courage or the imagination to take.

Richard O. Ristine
Lilly Endowment, Inc.

Preface

This book brings together a unique cast of experts from the fields of early childhood and juvenile justice and from legal and judicial areas, as well as administrative and social services.

Neither early childhood intervention nor the postulate that such interventions might, in fact, alleviate juvenile delinquency and crime has ever been addressed in this manner. Given the importance of this topic, it was especially gratifying to see so many interested leaders and professionals participating.

Several very important things must come from this book. If we are to begin making changes, recommendations must be developed that *can* be implemented, and a model plan must be agreed on. The following facts will guide us in our work.

We *are accountable* for our children.

We *must be responsible* for their development.

We *are molders* of their futures.

We *are models* after which they pattern their lives.

The Book of Proverbs (22:6) observes: "train up a child in the way he should go and when he is old he will not depart from it." In this Old Testament verse, Solomon was speaking to parents. We too need to help parents with their very important roles. Juveniles are responsible for 23 percent of all offenses that would be crimes if committed by adults, according to the U.S. Department of Justice, Bureau of Justice Statistics, *Sourcebook of Criminal Justice Statistics* 1980 (p. 338). Fifteen-hundred teachers a month are being attacked by students, with resultant injuries serious enough to need medical attention, as reported by D. Biless, *National Safe School Study* (Research Triangle Institute, 1977). We are responsible for making the changes that will significantly improve these situations.

Since most of a child's learning ability and patterns are set in the first four or five years of life, we must recognize the importance of early love, nurturing, example, training, and discipline in setting later standards and values. We must also approach intervention, however, in a way that is consistent with our nation's beliefs and with protection of the family, even as we allow for necessary help to reach the child and family at the time of need. The time and contributions of the concerned professionals represented in this book are truly valuable.

Barbara J. Anderson
Indiana Department of Mental Health

Acknowledgments

This book is the product of the Juvenile Delinquency and Early Childhood Intervention Conference held in Indianapolis, Indiana, on May 7, 8, and 9, 1981. This book and that conference resulted from the substantial effort of many people.

The editors are especially grateful to the Indiana Criminal Justice Agency, whose generous grant made the conference and this book possible. Essential also was the support, through John Ransberg, of the Indiana Juvenile Justice and Delinquency Prevention Advisory Board. Sincere thanks are also due the Indiana Lawyers Commission for organizing the conference. To thank the commission is to thank the Lilly Endowment, whose support has nurtured the commission.

The staff of the Indiana Lawyers Commission—including Timothy Clark, Catherine O'Connor, and Michael Reed—and Barbara Anderson of the Indiana Department of Mental Health were indispensable to the success of the conference and therefore to the completion of this book.

We extend as well our gratitude to Jane Conley, a Notre Dame Law School student, for her help in drafting the introduction, to Diana Smith, who cheerfully and tirelessly typed through several drafts of the manuscript, and to several others of the Notre Dame Law School staff for their cooperation.

The heart of this book, of course, is the contribution of the conference participants, who came together to pool their ideas and test those of others while exploring issues of critical importance. Although the papers, reactions, and discussion have been significantly edited for this book, every effort was made to preserve their substance and flavor. The editors regret any errors and are solely responsible for them.

Early Childhood Intervention and Juvenile Delinquency

1 Introduction

Fernand N. Dutile
and Jane Conley

Juvenile crime in America is widespread, growing, and often violent. No one knows how much juvenile crime is actually committed, but juvenile arrest and court records are staggering.[1] In 1979—the most recent year for which complete figures are available—fourteen children aged ten or younger were arrested for murder or nonnegligent manslaughter, six for forcible rape, and eight for embezzlement.[2] For children over the age of ten the figures are, of course, much higher.

History of the Juvenile Court System

The first juvenile-court case in the United States occurred in 1899 in Cook County, Illinois. A father brought his son to the court with the complaint: "I am unable to keep him at home. Associates with bad boys. Steals newspapers, etc."[3] The court committed the boy, age eleven, to the Illinois Manual Training School Farm (where the quality of his associates may not have improved). At that time—1899—the United States already had sixty-five institutions for children convicted of criminal offenses.[4] By 1922, when Sheldon and Eleanor Glueck were beginning their now-classic search for the roots of juvenile delinquency with a study of cases in the Boston Juvenile Court records, one-thousand case histories had accumulated there.[5]

The legal basis of the juvenile-court system was the common-law doctrine of parens patriae, the view that the state, as the ultimate parent, has responsibility and therefore power over minors. The Court of Chancery in England asserted its jurisdiction over children on the basis of its interest in the child's welfare. The crown may have invoked this power most frequently as a means of getting control over the estates of wealthy orphans: It was a form of civil jurisdiction, as the English courts of equity did not presume to control children who had violated the criminal law. In America, the Gluecks in the 1934 study note that the juvenile court arose on the criminal side of the courts because of a revolt at the idea of trying children over age seven as criminals.[6]

The first juvenile court (Cook County's) was instituted to help and protect children: Roscoe Pound called it "the most significant advance in the administration of justice since the Magna Carta."[7] By 1966, the system was described by Justice Fortas, writing for the Supreme Court, as one in which a child would get "the worst of both worlds: neither the protection given an adult nor the solicitous care postulated for children."[8] By the 1980s the system was being called "one of our children's most vicious enemies."[9]

Recognition of the present problem and a desire to find a better solution brought together the participants in the May 1981 Conference on Juvenile Delinquency and Early Childhood Intervention in Indianapolis, organized by the Indiana Lawyers Commission. The conference had a threefold purpose: first, to examine the roots of juvenile delinquency to ascertain whether there is any reliable way to predict it; second, to debate whether any kind of early intervention in children's lives could be shaped so as to prevent it; and third, to assess the lawfulness and appropriateness of any such intervention.

Concerns for the Present

The Gluecks pioneered the studies in whether juvenile delinquency is predictable, and if so, what factors can be used to predict it and with what weight. They explored causes widely and thoroughly.[10] The contributors, as this book shows, have travelled all the avenues the Gluecks indicated, and sometimes others, in their search for general causes as follows: the influences of family, home, school, and society; physical factors ranging from slight learning disabilities to brain damage; and the interactions among these areas. Predictability of juvenile delinquency remains too uncertain to be called a science, despite all these efforts.

Brandt F. Steele (chapter 6) puts concern with juvenile delinquency into a perspective of six-thousand years. Such a perspective has its comforting aspects (that is, our society is not the result of a final degeneration of all values) but suggests that the best we can hope for is improvement, not solution. Even if prediction will not work, the causes of juvenile delinquency uncovered in the search for prediction can suggest ways to attack the problem.

Another early caution about predictability comes from Jay Lindgren (chapter 3): Not all childhood correlates of adult criminal behavior are necessarily causes of it, and if this is true of the "simpler" factors such as conflict in the home, it is truer of such complex factors as I.Q., sex, or race.

Family influences are generally agreed to be a strong factor in either disposing a child toward later delinquency or keeping him from it. As Dr. Steele puts it (see chapter 6), early mistreatment of children is an important matrix providing a fertile ground for all the other deleterious influences to take root and flourish. One of the few certainties in this otherwise uncertain field is that a strong bond with a loving parent is a factor in producing a child who will not become a delinquent. Whether the converse is true—that lack of such a bond is sure to produce delinquency—probably cannot be proved. There is always what David Gilman (chapter 6) calls an "X" factor—either God or magic. We know that child abuse tends to produce delinquency. Neglect may be worse: the child is rejected by neglect for reasons he cannot understand, while abuse is a form of acceptance, however painful. (A recent *Time* article suggests that dating couples may provoke each other to violence to "break through indifference."[11]) Dr. Steele (see chapter 6) noted that neglect of an infant prevents its cognitive development, because the child is left with no way of connecting "A" with "B," an essential step toward full humanity. As E.M. Forster said, "Only connect . . ."[12]

Beyond the obvious harm done a child who is abused, family influences have an effect on physical condition. Improved nutrition may prevent birth defects, as Mary Hughes of the March of Dimes attests (chapter 4). Other physical conditions that may be related to delinquency are eye and speech disorders. A study in San Bernardino County, California, showed that rebellion, defiance, low self-esteem, and hyperactivity may result from as simple a cause as poor eyesight. The county's delinquency-prevention coordinator claimed that a project to improve eyesight "reduced the rate of recidivism among juvenile participants by nearly eighty percent during its first six months."[13] Speech therapy might yield like results: Debilitating communicative disorders affect 84 percent of juvenile offenders, as compared with about 5 percent of the population as a whole.[14]

Environment, or society, is blamed for causing juvenile delinquency. Society is subjected to the general charge that it is in a state of normlessness, termed "anomie . . . a social condition in which traditional norms and rules lose their authority over behavior,"[15] and to such particular charges as Joseph Scott's description of environments in which antisocial behavior is a normal adaptation (chapter 3). Irving Lazar (chapter 5) agrees that delinquent behavior can be a reasonable response to an unreasonable life situation. Dr. Steele's six-thousand-year perspective lessens the weight one would give to social conditions as a cause of delinquency (see chapter 6). As David Gilman (see chapter 3) asserts, family and social conditions that produce criminals produce artists as well. Moreover, children from middle-class families as well as those from poorer backgrounds become delinquents, too. Compared with influences from family and school, the influence of "society" is too general.

As for the schools, Lawrence J. Schweinhart (chapter 8) reminds us that scholastic failure has always been demonstrated to be related to delinquency. Any program that improves a child's performance in school, therefore, will probably help him avoid delinquency. John Monahan (chapter 3) points out that if staying in school predicts less crime, perhaps we use that factor in terms of some prevention programs because we want to increase a child's performance at school for reasons having nothing to do with future criminal behavior. Stephen Chinlund's comment (chapter 5) can be applied to both schools and society: "We undervalue human service and overvalue technological efficiency. With each of these familiar distortions in values, the children suffer most."

The juvenile courts themselves have often added to the juvenile delinquency problem they were created to deal with. Although an exhaustive account of their failures was not included in the forward-looking view of this book, Judge Bazelon has charged elsewhere that their very existence impedes other solutions: "Because you [the court] act, no one else does."[16] Contributors to this book seek other, more effective means for combatting the problem.

Options for the Future

Since the causes of juvenile delinquency are myriad and complex, action taken to improve any of the factors contributing to juvenile delinquency will probably help in its prevention. Lawrence P. Schweinhart (see chapter 8) observes that a program need not be a delinquency-prevention program in order to prevent delinquency. After all, as John P. Conrad said (chapter 5), partial solutions are better than none.

Early intervention into children's lives, however, is a problematic concept. Jay Lindgren, who has administered programs affecting the lives of adolescents, makes a plea for constraint in early intervention (see chapter 3). At the threshold, to choose some children and not others for intervention (if prediction is reliable enough) is unfair to both groups. The contributors generally agree that to label children by choosing them for any kind of coercive program is undesirable. Those not chosen may need help but be left without it because they suffered in silence. David Bahlman asserts (chapter 3):

> We are positing intervention, namely, good, positive programs, only for children exhibiting negative characteristics or behaviors. But there are hundreds and thousands of other children not exhibiting these things, who, living lives of total misery, need the same intervention. We are saying, in a sense, that crime pays.

The unfairness leads directly to a consideration of the constitutional problems such choices would raise. Juvenile courts avoided these problems in the beginning by using the parens patriae model. *Kent* v. *United States,*[17] *In re Gault,*[18] *In re Winship,*[19] and other constitutional challenges to that attitude have been met by the passage of new Juvenile Court Acts in some states, granting children the rights to such constitutional protections as due-process adjudicatory hearings. (John P. Conrad (see chapter 5) maintains that the present juvenile-court system is too unpredictable, in any event.)

Many states have been slow to act in this regard, either in writing the laws or in observing them.[20] Dan Hopson (chapter 7) points out, however, that intervention for potential delinquency would raise the same constitutional and legal issues: equal protection and due process, as well as First Amendment and privacy.

Choosing children who are thought to be at risk of delinquency could also lead to malpractice suits similar to that in *Tarasoff* v. *Regents of University of California*.[21] (The possibilities are awesome: For example, John X was not chosen for a prevention program, and he murdered my sister. Mary Y was chosen by error and now cannot stay out of jail.) Perhaps any programs adopted should be voluntary, the community making the program available to the child who needs it or wants it. Before any compulsory intervention is considered, Dan Hopson observes (see chapter 7), prediction ability should be better than the present more-or-less fifty-fifty state. Kenneth Stroud (chapter 7) points out that since *Parham* v. *J.R.*,[22] a child has a protectible liberty interest that includes the right to be free of physical restraint and the right to be free of erroneous stigmatization. The effort to find a stigma-free term for children selected for an intervention program resulted in the suggestion of calling them "green giraffes," effectively spotlighting the impossibility of avoiding stigma. The need to avoid it is the reason any program developed to counter juvenile delinquency should not be so labeled.

The ideal program would embody what Barbara J. Anderson (see chapter 9) called, quoting Judge Sharp, *individualized equality*. The television program, "Mister Rogers' Neighborhood," whose assistant producer, Hedda Sharapan, is a contributor to this book, could be considered a noncoercive and beneficial intervention in the lives of viewers. Ms. Sharapan (chapter 8) speaks of its providing the feeling of personal support all people—not only children—welcome and need. John Conrad (see chapter 5) suggests that child-labor laws might be selectively repealed to allow some children as young as twelve to hold part-time jobs or that some kind of universal national service be established. Both of these suggestions are aimed at the idea of school improvement.

Jan McCarthy's suggestions (chapter 8) for a Family Support Center, a community service along the lines suggested by Dan Hopson, appear to avoid the constitutional and legal problems. Such service would need to be sold to the public, as D. Robert Webster warns (chapter 9), and would be expensive, but several contributors point out that if at all effective, the services would save money in the long run. Also, of course, programs to improve schools and health programs would be money well spent. As Cleon Foust (chapter 9) observes, "the bullet that will best hit the most of these conditions [those contributing to delinquency] is increasing family support in all respects. . . ."

Notes

1. F.J. Vandall, "The Use of Force in Dealing with Juveniles," *Criminal Law Bulletin* 17 (1981):124.

2. *Parade*, July 19, 1981.

3. W.S. White, "Statement," *Pepperdine Law Review* 6 (1979):597.

4. J.T. Sprowls, *Discretion and Lawlessness: Compliance in the Juvenile Court* (Lexington, Mass.: Lexington Books, D.C. Heath, 1980). p. 11.

5. S. Glueck and E. Glueck, *One Thousand Juvenile Delinquents* (Cambridge, Mass.: Harvard University Press, 1934), p. 4. (Average age of boys studied was thirteen years, five months. No girls were studied.)

6. Ibid., p. 15, note 19.

7. G. Schramm, Philosophy of the Juvenile Court," in *The Problem of Delinquency*, ed. S. Glueck, (Boston: Houghton Mifflin, 1959), p. 270.

8. *Kent* v. *United States*, 383 U.S. 541 (1966).

9. M. Marticorena, "Take my Child Please—A Plea for Radical Nonintervention," *Pepperdine Law Review* 6 (1979):639.

10. See chapter headings, in G. Schramm, *supra*, note 7, part 1, section 2.

11. *Time*, September 21, 1981, pp. 66-67.

12. E.M. Forster, *Howards End* (New York: Knopf, 1910), title page, pp. 197, 329.

13. *Justice Assistance News* 2, no. 5 (1981):9.

14. J.S. Taylor, "Speech-Language Services for Youthful and Adult Offenders," *Federal Probation* 44 (1980):37.

15. D.S. Elliott, S.S. Ageton, and K.J. Canter, "Integrated Theoretical Perspective on Delinquent Behavior," *Journal of Research in Crime and Delinquency* 16 (1979):3.

16. D. Bazelon, "Beyond the Control of the Juvenile Court," *Juvenile Court Journal* 21 (1970):42.

17. 383 U.S. 41 (1966).

18. 387 U.S. 1 (1967).

19. 397 U.S. 358 (1970).

20. J.T. Sprowls, *supra*, note 4.

21. 17 Cal. 3d 425, 551 P.2d 334, 131 Cal. Rptr. 14 (1976), *vacating* 13 Cal. 3d 177, 529 P.2d 553, 118 Cal. Rptr. 129 (1974).

22. 442 U.S. 584 (1979).

2

The Challenge

Cleon H. Foust

During the middle of the twentieth century, we relied for crime control on three strategies: deterrence, quarantine, and rehabilitation. We discovered later that rehabilitation did not work and perhaps could never work well in the prison environment. More recently, then, in the late sixties and early seventies, we abandoned rehabilitation and relied pretty much on deterrence and quarantine or incapacitation. The result is determinate sentencing, mandatory penalties, and longer prison terms. We are now discovering that even these do not seem to work very well.

The problem is that we have no new strategies and must rely to some extent on deterrence and quarantine and perhaps other strategies and must, therefore, try to improve their effectiveness.

In the meantime, however, we must develop a method for attacking the very roots of crime. As Judge Bazelon has said, "The root causes of crime are, of course, far more complex and insidious than simple poverty."[1] The basis of this book is the affirmative postulate that the discovery of and early intervention in the lives of children at risk can reduce delinquency and later criminality. Whether stated this way or in the negative, there are three subsumptions at issue. First, any personality tilt toward delinquency is generally acquired very early in childhood. Second, delinquent children tend to become delinquent adults. Third, if the children at risk of delinquency can be discovered and somehow diverted, ultimate criminality can be reduced.

The first proposition is one of child development. The second is sort of a longitudinal perspective, raising the inquiry whether those same quirks of personality sometimes discovered in the child at risk or already delinquent will later likewise produce adult deviant behavior. These two propositions have sufficient support in the literature to warrant provisional acceptance. We consider the third proposition equally important and are perhaps most interested in it.

For convenience, the third proposition resolves itself into two inquiries: First, how does one discover children who are either overtly manifesting delinquency tilt or are in peril of delinquency as indicated through objectively identifiable signals? Such at-risk children are defined, by at least two authorities, as those "with deviant parents, especially those parents with psychotic and criminal histories. Those with chronic aggressive behavior disorders. Those who have suffered very severe social, cultural, economic and nutritional deprivations. Those who have physical, temperamental or intellectual handicaps."[2] This definition satisfactorily identifies a cohort of children that we wish to talk about. Nonetheless, the questions remain: Who discovers or identifies children at risk? Physicians, schoolteachers, or social workers?

Second, on the assumption that discovery is possible, what strategies for remedial intervention are possible in a free society? The recently published *Standards for the Administration of Juvenile Justice*[3] defines *intervention* only in terms of public-authority intervention. Although a substantial number of children at risk will be delinquent children, status offenders, and the like (for which there is public authority to intervene) children at risk encompass a larger group, for which there is no public authority to intervene. Indeed, the use of public authority, even when possible, may be inadvisable.

In discussing intervention, therefore, we wish to include voluntary and consensual strategies as well. The intervention we are interested in is purposeful action designed to at least influence, reinforce, and where necessary, change the trend of infant and childhood development of those at risk.

We can describe a group of children who are at risk of becoming delinquent, and later, adult criminals. But whether we can now identify such children and influence their development positively raises crucial questions: Who discovers these children and by what criteria? Once at-risk children are discovered, who can intervene and with what remedial strategies, raising what legal and constitutional questions? If this book cannot suggest answers, we are ready to admit that at this time there is none.

Notes

1. D. Bazelon, "Crime: Toward a Constructive Debate," *American Bar Association Journal* 67 (1981):438, 442.

2. V.R. Eisenstein and W. Krasner, *Children at Risk* (Washington, D.C.: U.S. Government Printing Office, 1978) (U.S. Department of Health, Education, and Welfare National Institute of Mental Health—Research Grant MH-24152), p. 2. One might bracket the phrase "aggressive behavior disorders." Any chronic behavior disorder, whether aggressive or not, warns us of some risk and perhaps, therefore, the term *aggressive* is not necessary.

3. U.S. Department of Justice, Office of Juvenile Justice and Delinquency Prevention, *Report of the National Advisory Committee for Juvenile Justice and Delinquency Prevention* (1980), p. 171.

Part I
Prediction

3 Childhood Predictors of Adult Criminal Behavior

John Monahan

William James once observed that we cannot hope to write biographies in advance. While it is surely true that we cannot fill in all the details, there seems to be an abiding belief, William James to the contrary, that we can at least outline the general plot of people's lives before the stories unfold. Indeed, many believe that the first few chapters of a person's life—that is, infancy and childhood—incubate the themes that will be played out, for better or worse, in all the rest. Almost every modern psychological theory, from the superego deficiencies of the psychoanalysts to the modeling theory of the behaviorists, supports this belief.

Far from being the "crystal-ball" activity it sometimes is made to appear, prediction is part of normal life. The human race would not have survived as long as it has were our ancestors not adept at predicting in some rough and intuitive way what nature had in store for them (for example, that lions may bite, and falling rocks may crush those people below). The predictions of the movement of the stars and the rising of the tides were among the first scientific puzzles to preoccupy humankind. On a more contemporary level, much of our own lives is spent predicting how others will respond to us, and we to them, as lover, friend, or colleague. The prediction of harm is likewise pervasive: We drive through green lights only because we predict that cross-traffic will stop on the red.

We are concerned here with prediction of delinquent or criminal behavior. I will first consider some concepts in methods of predicting behavior, then selectively review the research on childhood predictors of delinquent or criminal behavior, with particular emphasis on violent forms of delinquency or crime, and finally I will address the area's central policy issues.

Core Concepts in Prediction

Predictor and Criterion Variables

The process of predicting any kind of behavior requires that a person be assessed at two points in time. At time one, the person is placed into certain categories believed, for whatever reason, to relate to the behavior one is in-

11

terested in predicting. If one is interested in predicting how well a person will do in college, the categories might be "grades in high school," "letters from teachers" (rated as "very good," "good," or "poor"), and "quality of the essay written for the application" (perhaps scored on a one-to-ten scale). These are all *predictor variables*, categories consisting of different levels presumed to be relevant to what is being predicted. For delinquent or criminal behavior, the predictor variables might include "frequency of past aggression," "broken home," or "parent's drug abuse."

At some specified time in the future—time two—one assesses whether the person has or has not done what was predicted. This entails assessing the person on one or more *criterion variables*. For predicting "success" in college, the criterion variables might be "college grades," or "class rank," or "whether or not the person got a job in the desired field" (scored simply as "yes" or "no"). For criminal or delinquent behavior, the criterion variables may include "self-report," "arrest," or "conviction" for crime, or involuntary commitment as "dangerous to others." They could also include professional or peer ratings of "aggressive behavior" or scores on psychological tests to measure aggression.

Outcome of Positive and Negative Predictions

Four statistical outcomes, displayed in table 3-1, can occur in making a prediction of any kind of future behavior. One can predict either that the behavior (in this case, crime or delinquency) *will occur* or that it *will not occur*. At the end of some specified time period, one observes whether the predicted behavior actually *has occurred* or *has not occurred*.

If one predicts that crime will occur and later finds that, indeed, it has occurred, the prediction is called a *true positive*. One has made a positive prediction that turned out to be correct. Likewise, if one predicts that crime will not occur, and it in fact does not, the prediction is called a *true negative*, since one has made a negative prediction of crime that turned out to be true. These, of course, are the two outcomes one wishes to maximize in making predictions.

Table 3-1
Four Possible Outcomes of Predictive Decisions

	Actual Behavior	
Predicted Behavior	Yes	No
Yes	True positive	False positive
No	False negative	True negative

There are also two kinds of mistakes that can be made. If one predicts that crime or delinquency *will* occur, and it does *not*, the outcome is called a *false positive*. One made a positive prediction that turned out to be incorrect or false. In practice, this kind of mistake may mean that a child has unnecessarily been put into a program to prevent an act of crime that would not have occurred in any event. If one predicts that crime will *not* occur and it *does* occur, the outcome is called a *false negative*. In practice, this kind of mistake often means that someone who is not put into a preventive program, or who is released from the program, commits an act of crime or delinquency in the community. Obviously, predictors of crime try to minimize these two outcomes.

Decision Rules

Decision rules, "guidelines for the handling of uncertainty,"[1] involve choosing a "cutting score" on some predictive scale, above which one predicts for the purpose of intervention that an event will happen. A cutting score is simply a particular point on some objective or subjective scale. When setting a thermostat to 68 degrees, for example, one establishes a cutting score for the operation of a heating unit. When the temperature goes below 68 degrees, the heat comes on, and when it goes above 68 degrees, the heat goes off. In the treatment of cancer, as another example, one might decide that if tests show that a patient has a 20 percent chance of having cancer, it is best to operate. The decision rule or cutting score would then be a 20-percent probablity: At more than that you operate; at less than that you do not. The beyond a reasonable doubt standard of proof in the criminal law is a cutting score for the degree of certainty a juror must have in order to vote for conviction. Conviction is to occur only if doubt is nonexistent or unreasonable. In civil law, on the other hand, the juror generally need only decide which of two parties to a suit has the preponderance of the evidence. Reasonable doubts can still remain. Clearly, the cutting score can be set anywhere and can vary with the purpose and consequence of the prediction.

Where the cutting score is set determines the ratio of true-to-false positives. If the cutting score is set very low (for example, more crime-potential than the average child), there will be many true positives but many false positives also. If it is set very high (for example, 90 percent likely), there will be fewer false positives but fewer true positives as well.

It should be noted that the cutting score also determines the ratio of true positives and true negatives predicted and, therefore, the *absolute number* of successful predictions. If the decision rule is such that the cutting score is set very high, one will correctly identify most of the children who will not be criminal but at the expense of missing many of those who will be. Likewise, if the cutting score is low, one will correctly identify most of the children who will be criminal but at the cost of misidentifying many who would be safe.

These, then, are some of the core prediction concepts that should be kept in mind in evaluating the prediction research that follows.

Illustrative Research on Childhood Predictors of Adult Violence

One survey[2] reviewed 1,500 references to violent crime in psychiatric literature, interviewed over 750 professionals who dealt with violent persons, and retrospectively analyzed over 1,000 clinical cases to ascertain the most cited childhood predictors of adult violence. The authors reported that the four "early warning signs" were fighting, temper tantrums, school problems, and an inability to get along with others. The child, in other words, is indeed father or mother to the adult.

Based on discussions with large groups of psychiatrists and psychologists, Goldstein[3] concluded that the "agreed upon" predictors of adult violent crime were "a childhood history of maternal deprivation, poor father identification, or both; nocturnal enuresis; possibly fire setting; violence towards animals; and brutalization by one or both parents."[4] Diamond[5] comments that the conclusion of the clinicians cited by Goldstein represents the sum total of our present "scientific" knowledge concerning predictive factors of murderous violence:

> Yet I have repeatedly found some, and sometimes all of these predictive factors in individuals who have never committed even the slightest harm act, let alone assault or murder. And I have examined offenders who have committed the extraordinarily brutal acts of great violence and lethality who possessed none of these factors.[6]

In one of the most famous studies of the childhood correlates of later criminal behavior, *Unraveling Juvenile Delinquency*,[7] Sheldon and Eleanor Glueck claimed that these factors—supervision by the mother, discipline by the mother, and cohesiveness of the family—were predictive of later crime in young adolescent boys. This research, however, is among the most methodologically criticized in all of criminology, and there appears to be a consensus that the practical utlity of the Glueck factors in predicting criminality is marginal at best.

A 1977 longitudinal study by Lefkowitz, Eron, Walder, and Huesman entitled *Growing Up To Be Violent*[8] followed a sample of over four hundred males and females in Columbia County, New York, from ages eight to nineteen. Using peer ratings, parent ratings, self-report, and a personality test to measure aggressive behavior, Lefkowitz and his co-workers found that "aggression at age 8 is the best predictor we have of aggression at age 19, irrespective of I.Q., social class, or parents' aggressiveness."[9] Several other variables, among them the father's upward social mobility, low identification of the child with its parents, and a preference on the part of boys for watching violent television programs, were statistically significant predictors of aggression at age nineteen. Boys who, in the third grade, preferred television programs such as "Gunsmoke" or "Have Gun, Will Travel" were rated by their peers ten years later as three times as aggressive as boys who, in the third grade, preferred "Ozzie and Harriet," "I Love Lucy," or "Lawrence Welk." What is not clear from the study is why an eight-year-old boy would prefer "Lawrence Welk" to "Have Gun, Will Travel" in the first place.

McCord[10] reported in 1979 on a thirty-year follow-up of 201 boys who participated in the Cambridge-Somerville Youth Project between 1939 and 1945. She found that 36 percent of the incidence of later violent criminality could be accounted for by childhood predictive factors. "The boys who lacked supervision, whose mothers lacked self-confidence, who had been exposed to parental conflict and to aggression were subsequently more convicted for personal crimes.[11]

In what has become the most influential criminological research of the past decade,[12] Wolfgang[13] and his co-workers obtained information on all boys who, born in Philadelphia in 1945, lived there at least between their tenth and eighteenth birthdays. Of the 9,945 boys studied, 3,475, or 35 percent, had at least one recorded contact with the police by age 18. The Wolfgang group found that the variables of race and socioeconomic status (SES) were most strongly associated with reported delinquency: 29 percent of the whites, but 50 percent of the nonwhites, and 26 percent of the higher SES, but 45 percent of the lower SES boys had an offense record.

Six hundred and twenty-seven boys—6 percent of the sample and 18 percent of the total number of offenders—were responsible for over one-half of all offenses committed. Chronic offenders—defined as those who committed five or more offenses—in the cohort had a greater number of residential moves, lower I.Q. scores, a greater percentage classified as retarded, and fewer grades completed than did either the nonchronic or the one-time offenders, even when race and SES were held constant.[14]

Wolfgang has updated his research to include data on the subjects up to age thirty.[15] Only 5 percent of the subjects had an arrest record only as an adult (that is, after age eighteen but not before). While most juvenile offenders (61 percent) avoid arrest on reaching adulthood, the chances of being an adult offender are almost four times greater for one with a juvenile record than for one without. While 6 percent of the sample were "chronic" offenders by age eighteen, 15 percent were chronic by age thirty. The probability of future arrest varied directly with the incidence of past arrest: The probability of a fifth arrest (for any crime) given four priors was .80; the probability of an eleventh arrest given ten previous arrests was .90. The probability of a fifth *serious* (or index) offense with four prior arrests was .36; the probability of an eleventh serious offense given ten previous arrests was .42.

One of the best known and surely one of the most sophisticated longitudinal studies of the development of delinquency and crime is the Cambridge Study of Farrington and West.[16] The researchers studied 411 males contacted in 1961 and 1962 when they were eight and nine years of age. It was "overwhelmingly a traditional British white working class sample."[17] The boys were given tests in school at ages eight, ten, and fourteen and were interviewed at ages fifteen, eighteen, and twenty-one. Their parents were interviewed at home at regular intervals, and their teachers also completed questionnaires. Records of criminal and delinquent behavior were obtained from the Criminal Record Office in London.

About one-fifth (20.4 percent) of the boys were convicted of some delinquency offense between their tenth and seventeenth birthdays. The results of the predictive analysis, although very complex, can be summarized fairly straightforwardly: Only two behavioral measures and five background measures were independently predictive of delinquency. The delinquents were more likely than the nondelinquents to have been rated "troublesome" and "daring" during primary school. They also tended to come from poorer families, from larger-sized families, to have parents who were themselves criminal, to have parents who used harsh methods of child rearing, and to have a low I.Q. The more harsh the child rearing, the more violent the delinquency. Aggression at age eight was strongly related to aggression at age eighteen.

When these background factors were retrospectively combined to determine the extent to which they would have predicted future delinquency, a "vulnerable group" was identified, of whom about 50 percent became delinquent. This was only slightly better than making predictions on the grounds of teacher ratings of "troublesomeness" alone. While the seeds of delinquency can often be noticed in school, the school experience itself did not appear to have any positive or negative effect on later delinquency. Contact with the juvenile-justice system, however, did seem to have an effect: Self-reported delinquency significantly *increased* after conviction for delinquency.

Farrington[18] and his fellow researchers tried to determine why criminal fathers tend to have criminal sons. They found no evidence that criminal fathers encouraged their sons to commit crime. The major difference between convicted fathers and unconvicted ones was that the convicted fathers exercised poorer supervision over their sons.

Felthaus[19] reported a retrospective interview study of 149 people admitted to a military psychiatric unit, some with a history of serious assaultive behavior and others without. They were interviewed about various aspects of their childhoods in an effort to determine which factors differentiated the two groups. Members of the Aggressive Psychiatric Sample, compared with those of the Nonaggressive Sample, were significantly more likely to report having a variety of fights and violent outbursts, being suspended and truant from school, having frequent headaches and temper tantrums, setting uncontrolled fires, being cruel to animals, and experiencing enuresis beyond nine years of age. These last three factors form the triad often referred to in the literature. Further, the Aggressive Psychiatric Sample person was more likely to have an alcoholic father, to have received corporal punishment by both the mother and the father, and in particular, to have received blows to the head by both parents, often resulting in a loss of consciousness. Felthaus notes that these items "should not be considered as pathognomonic correlates of aggression. One would expect, however, that a combination of several of these symptoms in a child indicates a burgeoning difficulty in controlling aggressive impulses which could worsen in his adolescent and adult years."[20]

Summary of the Research

Although it is difficult to summarize the conclusions of so many studies on such diverse populations, the various predictive factors fall into three clusters.

Cluster A: Parent Factors

Four factors involving a child's parents surface in several studies as relating to the child's later criminal or delinquent behavior: (1) criminality of the parents themselves; (2) lack of parental supervision of the child; (3) conflict and disharmony between the parents; and (4) parental use of harsh and physical techniques of child rearing.

Cluster B: Child Factors

Five factors relating to the child himself seem to emerge from several of the studies: (1) gender (males are much more likely to become criminal than females); (2) race (blacks are much more likely to become criminal than whites); (3) I.Q. (the lower the measured I.Q. the more likely is later criminality); (4) aggressive or impulsive temperament (the more aggressive, impulsive, or daring the child, the more likely is later criminality); and (5) age at onset of delinquency (the younger the child when first exhibiting delinquent behavior, the more likely that behavior will continue throughout life).

Cluster C: School Factors

Both (1) the more interpersonal difficulties and (2) the more academic difficulties experienced at school, the more likely the child will later commit a crime.

To be sure, individual studies did report other factors that anticipated criminal behavior, but these three clusters seem the most persistent childhood correlates of adult criminal behavior.

How accurate, in terms of true and false positives, are these factors in predicting later crime and delinquency? Most studies do not report their data in this form, since they are really reports of so-called postdictions rather than predictions. They assessed children, then waited to see who later became criminal, and finally went back to see which of the childhood factors would have been useful as predictors. Farrington's Cambridge study[21]—surely one of the best of the prediction studies—indicates that it would have been possible, at best, to identify a high-risk group of children of whom approximately half would have been true positive and half false positive predictions of later crime. Two things need to be emphasized here: These are predictions of crime in general, and not of violent crime (predictions of violent crime would be much less accurate), and they are predictions among randomly chosen groups of children, not among children with extensive histories of involvement with the law (predictions of crime—of future arrest—among children with extensive criminal histories would be much more accurate).

The selection of predictive factors for actual use raises ethical and policy issues. For example, I would not use race or SES as predictors of violent crime, even though they do empirically relate to its occurrence. Barbara Underwood, in a *Yale Law Journal* article entitled, "Law and the Crystal Ball,"[22] urged, along the lines of Mr. Lindgren's remarks, that predictors not within the power of the individual to change—like age— be avoided. On the other hand, if staying in school is a predictor of less crime, perhaps one can use that factor in a prevention program. Even if that factor has nothing to do with crime, one is not hurting the child. If *better* school performances predicted more crime, however, one would not take that factor into account, since one does not want to worsen school performance.

Some Implications for Early-Intervention Programs

Does the existing research provide sufficient information on the childhood predictors of adult crime to justify preemptive interventions? My answer is twofold: (1) the issue is one of public policy—that is, of weighing benefits and costs—rather than one of science; and (2) from my own public-policy perspective, the answer depends on what early-intervention programs one is talking about. (Our predictive ability seems good enough for voluntary programs, for example, but not for coercive ones.[23])

A mental-health professional, a sociologist, or anyone else predicting that a child—absent some form of intervention—will become a delinquent, is really making three separate assertions:

1. the child has certain characteristics
2. these characteristics are associated with a certain probability of the child's becoming criminal
3. this probability is sufficiently high to justify preventive intervention, that is, the decision rule should be such that intervention occurs.

The first two of these assertions are scientific ones, whose truth or falsity can be established through research. It is possible to prove that a child does or does not have the characteristics claimed, and one can present data on their association with later crime.

The third assertion—one of a different sort—is not capable of scientific proof. It is a social policy statement that must be arrived at through the political process. This entails a weighing of the *costs* of the intervention to the false positives—that is, the children who are erroneously predicted to need it—as well as the potential *benefits* of the intervention to the true positives.[24]

What are the costs of early-intervention programs? The two most frequently cited are labeling effects, that is, the effects on the child's self-concept of being directly or indirectly labeled a predelinquent, and the widening of the net of social control, allowing government broader authority to intervene in the lives of people (children, in this case) who have not been convicted of crime.

How real are these costs? That is, how likely are prevention programs to have harmful labeling effects and to expand governmental power in insidious ways? Unfortunately, there are no clear answers. Indeed, the existence and severity of labeling effects and of net-widening are possibly the two most controversial issues in delinquency prevention today.[25]

What are the benefits of delinquency-prevention programs? Here, too, research offers little assistance. A large number of studies have found no difference, in terms of reduction of future crime, between children exposed to prevention programs and those not exposed.[26] Yet there are some bright spots on the horizon.[27] After all, the research reflects intervention that has been done, not the kind of intervention that is possible.

So we are faced with these following three facts:

1. At best only half the children we identify as in need of early-intervention programs are actually in such need.
2. The negative effects of the intervention programs are unknown.
3. The positive effects of intervention programs are also unknown, but in the past have tended to be minimal.

Nonetheless, we should not throw up our hands and do nothing. Programs could perhaps be devised that would not hurt the false positives and would help the true positives. The lesson to be derived from the research on delinquency prediction and delinquency prevention is not one of despair, but one of caution.

Notes

1. American Psychiatric Association, *Clinical Aspects of the Violent Individual* (Washington, D.C.: American Psychiatric Association, 1974).

2. B. Justice, R. Justice, and J. Kraft, "Early Warning Signs of Violence: Is a Trait Enough?," *American Journal of Psychiatry* 131 (1974):457-459.

3. R. Goldstein, "Brain Research and Violent Behavior," *Archives of Neurology* 30 (1974):1-18.

4. Ibid., p. 27.

5. B. Diamond, "The Psychiatric Prediction of Dangerousness," *University of Pennsylvania Law Review* 123 (1974):439-452.

6. Ibid., p. 444.

7. S. Glueck and E. Glueck, *Unraveling Juvenile Delinquency* (New York: The Commonwealth Fund, 1950).

8. M. Lefkowitz, E. Eron, L. Walder, and L. Huesman, *Growing Up To Be Violent* (New York: Pergamon, 1977).

9. Ibid., p. 192.

10. J. McCord, "Some Child Rearing Antecedents to Criminal Behavior in Adult Men," *Journal of Personality and Social Psychology* 37 (1979):1477-1486.

11. Ibid., p. 1485.

12. See G. Geis and R. Meier, "Looking Backward and Forward: Criminologists on Criminology and a Career," *Criminology* 16 (1978):273-288.

13. M. Wolfgang, R. Figlio, and T. Selin, *Delinquency in a Birth Cohort* (Chicago: University of Chicago Press, 1972).

14. Ibid., p. 248.

15. See M. Wolfgang, "From Boy to Man—From Delinquency to Crime," *National Symposium on the Serious Juvenile Offender* (Minneapolis, 1977).

16. D.P. Farrington and D.J. West, "The Cambridge Study in Delinquency Development" (1980).

17. Ibid., p. 137.

18. D. Farrington, G. Gundry, and D. West, "The Familial Transmission of Criminality," *Medical Science Law* 15 (1975):177-186.

19. A. Felthaus, "Childhood Antecedents of Aggressive Behaviors in Male Psychiatric Patients," *Bulletin of the American Academy of Psychiatry and Law* 8 (1980):104-110.

20. Ibid., pp. 107-108.

21. D.P. Farrington and D.J. West, *supra*, note 16.

22. B. Underwood, "Law and the Crystal Ball: Predicting Behavior With Statistical Inference and Individualized Judgment," *Yale Law Journal* 88 (1979):1408-1448.

23. Interventions are often "voluntary" in name only (for example, when a child is given the "option" of family counseling or custody). The true test of voluntariness is whether the child can say "no" and walk out the door. Even then, there is a cost: The next time, the child will not be given an option.

24. J. Monahan and D. Wexler, "A Definite Maybe: Proof and Probability in Civil Commitment," *Law and Human Behavior* 2 (1978):37-42.

25. M. Klein, "Deinstitutionalization and Diversion of Juvenile Offenders: A Litany of Impediments,' in N. Morris and N. Tonry, *Crime and Justice: An Annual Review of Research* (Chicago: University of Chicago Press, 1979), pp. 145-202.

26. K. Sechrest, S. White, and E. Brown, *The Rehabilitation of Criminal Offenders: Problems and Prospects* (Washington, D.C.: National Academy of Sciences, 1979).

27. Ibid.

Commentary

Jay Lindgren

As a practitioner who has administered several programs affecting adolescent children, I am most concerned with the practical application of the empirical knowledge Professor Monahan presented for social policy and programs. His presentation, a concise analysis and summary of the key empirical findings in delinquency prediction literature, establishes a most appropriate framework for the beginning of our deliberations. My first reaction, similar to his conclusion, is that caution—indeed, even constraint—is the most appropriate rallying cry for a deliberation of early childhood intervention.

How to intervene intelligently depends, of course, on what we hope to change by intervening and, as importantly, with whom we plan to intervene. Only through balancing what we intend to accomplish, how we intend to do it, and with whom, can we reach any final conclusions. Like Professor Monahan, I do not despair but suggest that we must proceed very cautiously.

This commentary first examines the practicality of the persistent childhood correlates of adult criminal behavior identified from the literature by Professor Monahan. Second, I will then stress several of the general themes that emerge from the cohort and longitudinal studies presented by Professor Monahan. Third, I will briefly identify lessons from a different type of literature, which assists in predicting how the organizations or agencies we design might perform. Finally, I will suggest operational principles crucial to developing intervention models.

Professor Monahan has identified three clusters of childhood correlates of adult criminal behavior: parent factors, child factors, and school factors. First it must be emphasized that these are correlates or associations, not necessarily causes. For example, conflict and disharmony in the home or lack of supervision may in fact be a result of other, deeper factors. Lack of supervision, one of the examples Professor Monahan used, might be caused by a single parent's illness or caused by the fact that the family attempting to raise the child is overwhelmed by the child's frustrating behavior problems. Indeed, it could simply be parental indifference. Each of these possibilities—and we could add many others—identifies different causal relationships requiring a very different kind of response.

If there is complexity with these fairly straightforward social situations, purposeful intervention with the even more complex personal factors presented becomes more difficult. Take, for example, I.Q. Knowing a child's I.Q. may sensitize a teacher's approach or expectations with regard to a particular child. Such knowledge may also set up a self-fulfilling prophecy. Almost by definition, I.Q. is not open to intervention or change. Although we know that males and members of racial minorities are more likely to get into trouble, neither sex nor race is a factor that can be changed. A deeper analysis is required: What is it about our social structure, or more specifically, what is it about the experience of minorities and males that might explain the association with later delinquency?

Nonetheless, there are factors Monahan identifies that are behavior-related (for example, school performance and aggressive behavior). When these factors are identified, some types of purposeful intervention may be appropriate.

Even here, however, some difficult ethical and legal problems arise. The sanctity and privacy of the home, on the one hand, and, on the other, the desire to detect and protect children from parental aggression and, particularly, brutal treatment, are competing values in our society.

A young man whom I shall call John expressed a part of this conflict to me. Following a series of runaways from a variety of placements, John wanted to return home to a family that had all the factors mentioned in Professor Monahan's family cluster. The correctional wisdom at that time was that John had failed our most recent attempt to help him and, therefore, we could not reward his irresponsible behavior by giving him what he wanted, another chance at home. Questioned about his motives for returning home, he said, referring to his family, "They might be shitty, but at least they're mine."

I recently participated in a parole revocation hearing involving a young woman going through the same kind of decision-making. For several years she had been in a variety of out-of-home placements, each one ending with running away, sometimes for several months. Her last recorded criminal-level offense, two years previously, had involved shoplifting a $13. sweater that was immediately returned. All of her offenses following that theft involved her avoidance of the answer we were coming up with for her.

The purpose of intervention, it appears, was the state's attempt to protect, more specifically to provide a chastity belt for this young woman. The underlying concern seemed to be promiscuity, although neither this problem nor this purpose was articulated or documented. Indeed, even if documentation of promiscuity existed, little was being done about it. The insistence on her being in a better place—a place without the correlates of adult criminality—resulted in driving her further underground because she now not only ran away but also had to hide from the authorities. She was driven into situations worse than those in which she would have remained had she been left alone. She was now with people who were willing to hide children from the justice system.

School factors as well as home factors are associated with future criminality. Although there is some correlation between I.Q. and delinquency, a person's I.Q. in itself does not yield much information useful to predicting future criminal behavior. Despite associations, many bright people end up in prison, and many intellectually dull people are productive and contributing citizens. I.Q. measures often distinguish between performance I.Q. and verbal I.Q. In my experience, delinquent children often have a high or at least average performance I.Q. with a verbal I.Q. below average. My hypothesis is that as our society has produced a greater volume of written and spoken information and a greater dependency on the ability to deal with that material, it has become more and more difficult for people weaker in the verbal area to feel adequate or competent.

A fifteen-year-old young man whom I shall call Mike expressed this issue very clearly to me. A chronic delinquent involved mostly in property offenses such as car thefts, Mike came to my attention because of an assault on a schoolteacher. I participated in a group discussion involving him and several other juvenile and young-adult offenders.

The atmosphere that night was crackling with anger and recrimination. Mike had been truant from school that day, which upset the older members of the group. Most of them were dropouts, and they were not willing to see one of the younger people in the program go the way they had. The group was very important to Mike, who became extremely upset as they expressed their frustration. As he wept, he described his school experience.

> My math class is easier than my friends' little brothers' and sisters' who are in grade school math. When I sit in my English class, the teacher goes around and asks kids to read out loud, but always skips me because if I attempt to read out loud, I am going to make a fool of myself. She knows that and all the kids in school have figured that out, too.
>
> I am stupid. Why try in school? If I try their way, I will just look like a dumb shit to everybody. But if I act tough, at least a few kids in school look up to me.

Many kids in our school systems have concluded that they confront this existential choice. Yet I have camped, worked on cars, and discussed nature and the universe with Mike and have learned from him. He is not dumb!

As Professor Monahan points out, the family and the school are critical. There is, however, no simple way to reconcile children and youth in conflict with these complex institutions or to make these institutions more responsive. Many of our solutions further sever the already fragile relationship. Yet attempts to prevent must center on these interactions.

Longitudinal studies offer the most valid prediction information, particularly Farrington's study in England and Wolfgang's in Philadelphia.[1] Some of the conclusions in those studies are not immediately helpful in developing intervention models but are important as we consider the proper role of prediction for model development. First, a high proportion of adolescents engage in delinquent behavior. In the Farrington study, more than 20 percent were convicted and, in the Wolfgang group—a random selection—35 percent were arrested. Gold's Flint, Michigan study,[2] also randomly selected, used self-disclosure and indicated that 80 percent of the youth interviewed engaged in delinquent behavior. Thus, of the perhaps 80 percent of youth who engage in delinquent behavior, 35 percent will be arrested, and 20 percent will be convicted. In many ways, delinquent behavior is normal adolescent behavior.

However, these studies also point out that most of these youth discontinue delinquent behavior, and the major dynamic seems to be simply growing older. There appears to be little association between the discontinuation of delinquent or criminal behavior and purposeful intervention. Indeed, as Professor Monahan has pointed out in one of the studies, contact with purposeful intervention may exacerbate the problem rather than ease it.

Another important theme in these studies, much stressed these days, is that a hard-core group continues to repeat. Wolfgang concluded that 6 percent of the Philadelphia youth accounted for over half of the total cohort offenses. The Gold study indicated that 17 percent of the youth accounted for over half the offenses reported by that particular group. This hard core commits future offenses with a much higher probability and has an even higher probability of committing serious offenses.

I draw three conclusions from these studies, conclusions not yielding easy direction for intervention. First, the best predictor of future criminal behavior is past criminal behavior. Second, normal maturation is the best change agent, but we have no technique for accelerating it. Indeed, many of our attempts hinder normal maturation. At best, we can support it. Finally, with regard to the serious and chronic group, even though we can identify 6 percent to 17 percent of the most persistent offenders, that is too large a group in most communities for special programs or differential policies. Moreover, even with the identified group, if we try to predict how many of them will go on to commit serious crimes—and Wolfgang has done this with his 6 percent—the odds are about even of predicting a false or a true positive for future index crimes.[3]

Finally, another form of inquiry helps inform our predictions of how agencies and agency personnel will respond and support a posture of constraint. This literature comes out of the history of institutional reform and from studies of organizational development.[4] Programs established to provide alternatives to outmoded, inhumane, or ineffective methods tend to gravitate away from the targeted group or perhaps miss the group entirely. This is sometimes referred to as "creaming." Those persons controlling entrance into and exit from programs seek clients who are going to be the least likely to cause problems or embarrassment, those with whom they can be the most successful. Programs set up as substitutes for existing methods of intervention usually end up as supplements. More and more people come under the net of coercive social control. This has held true in both mental-health and criminal and juvenile justice and must be kept in mind in any discussion of intervention. We may easily end up dealing with children and youth who do not need our intervention.

It seems to me that a first, superordinate principle flows from all of this research. In trying to identify persons likely to commit offenses, we should require predictive variables that describe behavior for which the youth can be held legally culpable or personally responsible. The agency designed to do that is the juvenile court which, despite all of its problems, is the fairest and perhaps most empirically precise method. The court operates in an adversary setting, establishes that a particular act occurred and was intended, examines the seriousness of the act and its consequences, and weighs the age of the person and the history of prior acts in considering whether coercive intervention should occur. It is a simple-minded approach, but one that is often forgotten.

When we decide to intervene with particular individuals or groups, the cutting scores, as Professor Monahan refers to them, must be kept as high as possible. We should maximize the number of true negatives and minimize the number of false positives at the cost of missing some of the false negatives. That, it seems to me, is not only just but is empirically sound.

This is a particularly important emphasis, given the current national get-tough-on-kids movement. It is easy these days to allow the desire to eliminate the false negative to continue to lower the cutting score for prospective action, whether it be prevention, treatment in the community, or removal and institutionalization.

I would urge that deliberations of prevention or early intervention not attempt to target particular individuals or groups of individuals. Primary prevention, when attempted, should be from a situational rather than personal model. Such a model emphasizes the biological and social environment that children and youth grow up in over intervention with the individual. It stresses physical well-being and seeks to provide the best kind of social psychological support possible, preferably within the family. It targets resources to the neighborhood schools and to other normal everyday agencies and seeks to improve their fairness, their safety, and their respect for the differences and for autonomy of the individual and to reinforce the mutual obligation of individuals as members of a community. This is not a mollycoddling or blame-society approach. Focusing on the situation in which children grow up instead of targeting individuals makes the inclusion of false positives irrelevant, because the action will benefit all, not only the delinquent.

This does not require that we overlook the personal development of individuals or specific misbehavior that is noncriminal.[5] Intervention with regard to the nuisance, particularly when it does not interfere with others, should be requested, either by the juvenile or the family. Such a system will, by having dropouts, foster more responsive and effective services.

When there is a problem of specific behavior, the service ought to be immediate and strive to represent an authentic response. Authentic responses require programs with young, energetic, and idealistic staff. This is best done in private, nonprofit agencies located in the community.

Dealing with specific kinds of behavior other than criminal requires respect for how the individual with the problem defines the problem. The purpose of a service is not established when an agency staff superimposes a definition of a problem but rather when the family or child describes the problem in relation to agency staff. The agency must be close, on a neighborhood, not city or state level. It must be accessible by telephone, provide service when there is a request, and be willing to go out into the community to bring people to it or to more specialized services when indicated. It must have a friendly atmosphere.

Maintaining friendly agencies requires penetration by the youth's peers and parents so that loved ones are involved with the source of control of the program. It should not be run by the state or the federal government; they may be in the background, offering basic support, technical assistance, and specialized services, but they should not administer the front-line services.

I am not advocating a permissive approach with children and youth. There remain youth who do and will again commit criminal-level offenses, offenses that interfere with the rights of others. These youths often do require a coercive intervention. The resources for such interventions, however, are expensive and finite and therefore are and should be reserved for known serious and chronic offenders. Such intervention must be preceded by the due process of law provided through the juvenile court. What proceeds from there should be proportional to the harm done by the individual, not what is predicted as future harm or what the youth "needs" in the way of preventive services.[6] To the extent possible, within the parameters of the court orders, such youths too should have before, during, and after the court-ordered intervention full access to the preventive programs we develop.

In summary, prediction of future delinquency or criminal behavior is an empirically weak and probably inevitably corrupting purpose on which to develop a helping agency. Such purposes and claims may have political value for establishing social or economic support for programs. To the extent that an agency operates with prevention as a primary mission on which to provide services to individual children and youth, however, we have failed to learn from the lessons of the past and will develop programs that undermine democracy, freedom, pluralism, and respect for the dignity and autonomy of the individual. We are much more likely to assist and support the positive future that is in children and youth when we provide for them exactly what we would want for a loved one.

Notes

1. See J. Monahan, "Childhood Predictors of Adult Criminal Behavior," chapter 3.

2. M. Gold, *Delinquent Behavior In An American City* (Belmont, Calif.: Brooks/Cole, 1970).

3. F.E. Zimring, "American Youth Violence: Issues and Trends," in N. Morris and M. Tonry, *Crime and Justice: An Annual Review of Research* (Chicago: The University of Chicago Press, 1979), pp. 67-107.

4. See, e.g., D.J. Rothman, *Conscience and Convenience* (Boston: Little Brown, 1980); Minnesota Department of Corrections Research Information Systems, "The Effect of the Availability of Community Residential Alternatives to State Incarceration on Sentencing Practices: The Social Control Issue," mimeographed (1977); E.J. Pawlak, "Differential Selection of Juveniles for Detention," *Journal of Research on Crime and Delinquency* (July 1977):152-165; A. Rutherford and R. McDermott, "Juvenile Diversion," *National Evaluation Program Phase I Summary Report* (U.S. Department of Justice, September 1976); F.E. Zimring, "The Court Employment Project" (report to the New York City Human Resources Administration, 1973); F.E. Zimring, "Measuring the Impact of Pretrial Diversion from the Criminal Justice System," *University of Chicago Law Review* 41 (1974):224-241; P. Lerman, *Community Treatment and Social Control* (Chicago: The University of Chicago Press, 1975); P. Lerman, "Trends and Issues in the Institutionalization of Youths in Trouble," *Crime and Delinquency* (July 1980):281-298; N. Morris, *The Future of Imprisonment* (Chicago: The University of Chicago Press, 1974), pp. 9-12; D. Miller, "Alternatives to Incarceration: From Total Institutions to Total Systems" (Ph.D. dissertation, The University of California Berkeley, 1980).

5. Rosenheim recommends a "normalizing perspective." See her very thoughtful discussion, "Notes on Helping Juvenile Nuisances," in M. Rosenheim, *Pursuing Justice for the Child* (Chicago: The University of Chicago Press, 1976), pp. 43-66.

6. See, e.g., F.E. Zimring, *Confronting Youth Crime: Report of the Twentieth Century Fund Task Force on Sentencing Policy Toward Young Offenders* (New York: Holmes and Meier, 1978); Institute of Judicial Administration, American Bar Association, *Juvenile Justice Standards: Juvenile Delinquency and Sanctions* (Cambridge, Mass.: Ballinger, 1980).

Roundtable

Bahlmann: Dr. Monahan, Jay Lindgren suggested a possible structure for an intervention program. What is your reaction?

Monahan: Although I have no argument with the structure, I am not hopeful, in the current political climate, of establishing the primary prevention programs he mentions. Indeed, the current political climate suggests movement in the opposite direction.

Scott: It seems as if we are blaming the victim. What if we examined the files of Indianapolis department stores and found that 96 percent of white shoplifters were turned over to the police versus 60 percent of black shoplifters or vice versa? The arrest record, which we have discussed using for prediction, would not reveal that kind of discretion. We seem to be designing programs with the idea that whites are the problem, or blacks are the problem, depending on which group has the higher proportion sent to the police station, as opposed to reality. As Jay Lindgren points out, maybe 80 or 90 percent of all kids are engaged in antisocial behavior, but not all are arrested. I am concerned, in short, that arrest records and other so-called official statistics used as predictors say more about the reactors to certain behavior rather than the actors. On which side of this question are we going to intervene?

Conrad: I have always been skeptical of self-report studies. First, their data tend to be undifferentiated; that is, the delinquency involved falls into a large number of different categories. Second, some of the delinquency is extremely minor. In one English study, for example, some of the delinquency reported involved arrests for riding a bicycle without a rear light. That conduct is not ominous. One of the problems that results is an underrepresentation of the major kinds of delinquency.

Gilman: Race and class bias is endemic to our society, to delinquency, and to criminality in adults. It is endemic to correctional administrations, court organizations, prosecutorial services, defense services, and the like. We cannot discuss anything in this area without this assumption. Regardless of our model, race or class factors will motivate political decision-making in the identification process, whether or not they are articulated.

Shoplifting is a perfect example. The vast majority of shoplifting, I understand, is done by white, middle-class women in suburban areas. Ten percent is done by young people, but 90 percent of the arrests are of young people. An analysis of arrest records for shoplifting, therefore, suggests that all shoplifters are young people, which, in fact, is far from the case.

We must constantly be alert, therefore, to this element of irrationality; class and race biases continue to defeat a rational and humanistic response to the real issue.

Hopson: I am concerned about our use of prior violence as a predictor for future violence since, by definition, this conference is looking at the possibility of intervening with children who have not yet done anything. What do we know, if anything, about the behaviors of four-, five- and six-year-olds that predict their behavior as twelve-, thirteen-, and fourteen-year olds?

Monahan: Most studies looked at children when they were eight or nine. Any conduct prior to that time must be revealed in parental interviews. Indeed, some studies have interviewed mothers about complications during pregnancy and the like.

It is true that the best predictor of future crime is past crime and, if you eliminate past aggressive crime, the prediction becomes that much more difficult. Nonetheless, we do have some ability to predict the first arrest. For example, criminality of a parent would give some indication. The difficult question is whether the current level of predictive ability justifies preventive intervention, which is a social-policy question. For purely voluntary interventions, social services that people can take or not, we know enough. For interventions that are implicitly or explicitly coercive, our predictive ability is not good enough.

Often, interventions are voluntary in name only (for example, in diversion programs in which the child is given the option of family counseling or of going to jail). A program is truly voluntary if the child can simply say no and walk out the door. Even there, there is an implicit cost, namely, the loss of a similar option the next time the child gets into trouble.

Hopson: Is talk of choice on the part of three-, four- or five-year-old children realistic?

Monahan: Choice is not a very useful concept with three-year-olds. Obviously, choice becomes more realistic as age increases. Many of the predictive factors, like school performance, do not appear until the child is older than three. To be sure, some family factors will appear. As early as age two, for example, males exhibit more signs of aggressiveness than females, although, obviously, that does not mean they are violent. We can, therefore, make some distinctions among various groups at very early ages.

Lindgren: We do not want kids to begin developing records at the age of three.

Hopson: It depends on what is meant by record. Prevention requires assessment of data at an early age. We may conclude that behavior at age three, four, five, or six is not predictive and forget about prevention. But if the experts are able to predict behavior, we must ask the relevance of those data in terms of treating four-, five-, and six-year-olds.

Steele: John Conger's 1966 study[1] of a very large number of school children concluded that factors apparent in the records of children in kindergarten and the first two grades correlated with later juvenile-delinquent behavior. We do, therefore, have meaningful data about children four-and-one-half to five years old, at least.

Scott: This discussion has ignored environmental factors. For example, the antisocial behavior of a four-, five-, or six-year-old child could be adaptive, conforming behavior for that child's particular context. It may have nothing to do with antisocial character disorders. In certain neighborhoods, stealing a little bit, drinking a little bit, or whatever, is adaptive, conforming behavior. In such cases, will we treat the environment, the group context, the community context, and the family context, in which the child is operating, or will we, taking the child out of that context, treat him as maladaptive, as possessing a character disorder?

Moreover, many situations are difficult to predict. A person might get divorced and commit suicide next week; could that be predicted when he was five years old? If a kid's parents break up when he is a teenager, and he runs away from home, could that have been predicted when he was five years old?

Furthermore, what will follow this treatment? If a child is put into an institution, given treatment, and then returned to his former environment, we are likely to say that the institution succeeded but the child failed when he indulges in the same conduct that first brought him to the institution. We should not casually expect that such a child can rise above all of the forces and all of the conditions from which he came.

Gilman: We must not confuse intervention with prevention. Much intervention in the early lives of children has nothing to do with prevention and, according to some research, may increase future criminality rather than decrease it.

Scott: This might be due to the labeling concept.

Bahlmann: Are there factors other than prior criminal activity that might, at an early age, justify at least voluntary intervention, even at the risk of labeling? If so, is that factor school-oriented, for example, a learning disability, is it family-oriented, for example, abuse or neglect, or might it be the family structure, for example, the single-parent family? Could such factors justify at least current-state-of-the-art intervention and, if so, at what age?

Lindgren: When prediction is the motive, we do something because we fear something else will happen in the future. Such a motivation leads to more control and less voluntariness on the part of the subjects. We can intervene in matters like child abuse or neglect simply on the basis of what we know already, and do it for humane motives (that is, preventing children from being beaten or neglected).

Indeed, at some age, children should be given the choice to go back home and be beaten. This is not true, obviously, at earlier ages. But we remove an abused three-year-old from the home not to prevent him from hurting people in the future, but because we don't want him abused anymore.

Conrad: Child abuse and child neglect are obviously very serious indicators of future trouble of many different kinds. One isn't going to allow these to happen in a civilized society. How much farther, however, can one carry intervention on the basis of adversary conditions or suffering of the child?

Steele: As a physician, I have a different attitude toward predictions. Although only a relatively small proportion of the population will get serious poliomyelitis, we believe it worthwhile to give the vaccine. What is predicted is a risk, not an actual happening. Similarly, we can predict the risk of delinquency without predicting "Johnny" will commit a specific crime. This attitude views prediction and prevention from an angle other than that of absolute statistical rigidity.

Hollingsworth: We have gotten ourselves into a trap. The goal of prediction is the best or smallest set of predictors allowing an estimate of the possibility of certain conduct. Unfortunately, in discussing children, we no longer are talking about remedial intervention or proactive treatment. We are talking about trying to prevent. This is a very multistructured matter that cannot be reduced to one, two, three, or four best predictors.

Hopson: Our compulsory education laws, enacted a long time ago, were based on a prediction that children not attending school would be ignorant at age twenty-one and took away the decision-making power of the parents with regard to the education of their child.

An educated society reflects a very high value, and if nonviolent behavior on the part of twenty-one-year-olds is also of high value, and if our prediction of such behavior is as good as our prediction of ignorance, is there any significant difference between compulsory education and the intervention we are discussing?

Hollingsworth: The median reading level and math level of a person above twenty-one is below seventh grade; we have not been too successful in that area, therefore. Our intervention with regard to future delinquency must be more specific than compulsory education has been.

Bahlmann: The polio situation is quite different since it involves a one-dimensional vaccine aimed at one problem. Our problem involves family factors and child factors, and any intervention "vaccine" must be very specific.

Scott: We must remember that many delinquents are good readers, are well educated, and come from middle-class families. There may be twenty or thirty different factors accounting for juvenile delinquency. If we know that certain kinds of gang behavior result in the promotion of certain kinds of delinquency, why not treat that situation rather than deal only with the one kid who gets arrested, thus leaving the other thirty or forty kids on the street?

Hopson: Will you then allow us to intervene with the six-year-old boy about to be recruited by this gang even though he has not yet done anything wrong?

Scott: We should treat the gang. The six-year-old kid has not yet been touched. Why not reorient the gang?

Bahlmann: We are positing intervention, namely, good, positive programs, only for children exhibiting negative characteristics or behaviors. But there are hundreds and thousands of other children not exhibiting these things, who, living lives of total misery, need the same intervention. We are saying, in a sense, that crime pays.

Hopson: Prediction of crime pays.

Schweinhart: I have been involved over a period of years in longitudinal research showing that prediction and early intervention lead to a decrease in delinquent behaviors.

Society's problems are intertwined. Scholastic failure relates not only to delinquency but also to the personal environmental mix that we are concerned about. Scholastic failure is bad not only because of the damage it does to children and the problem it creates in school, but also because it is related to delinquency. Early-intervention programs preventing scholastic failure will also lead to a reduction in juvenile delinquency, but such programs can be justified on the basis of reducing scholastic failure alone.

Audience Member: As the only juvenile judge for a population of 82,000, and with no referees, and with probation officers carrying a caseload of about six hundred, I would ask what other form of coercion there is except that under the due process of the judicial system? Maybe I can use it. When I see a family in which the parents are consistently delinquent, I can generally assume that the children will follow suit, although occasionally something like athletics might pull one child out of the channel. Nonetheless, intervention is difficult because the law makes removal of the child from its family a last resort.

Every other device, however, is expensive. My entire budget for juries and for counseling is used up after only six months of the budget year. Regrettably, any marvelous ideas that you or I have will not survive in the practical world in which taxpayer support is required. The money is not there and will not be for a number of years.

Audience Member: The discussion has suggested that we cannot accelerate maturation, but an evaluation of drug-abuse-prevention programs that I have seen contradicts that statement.

Indiana has introduced a program, in existence elsewhere for about twenty-five years and validated by the National Institute of Mental Health, dealing with children in kindergarten through third grade. Over 150 research articles support the program's productiveness in the prevention of destructive behavior. Is not this pull-out program for young people identified as high risk an appropriate one?

Lindgren: I have no problem in identifying on the basis of conduct. My concern involves identifying through things other than behavior. Race has been suggested as a high correlate but is not a proper reason for any coercive intervention. Since, as Professor Monahan has indicated, predictions based on prior offenses are most accurate, our limited resources are best focused on those. Moreover, prior offenses present the fairest method of targeting. We should use the past, and not the future, to justify what we are doing now.

The family should participate in the child's fate. Too often, we see the state as a substitute for the parents rather than participating with the parents so that the family does not feel pushed out. I favor family counseling and treatment.

Audience Member: We need a positive campaign urging parents, teachers and Sunday school teachers, neighbors, and relatives to impress on children that we have a great country, that stable families are needed to keep it great, and that good citizens do not cheat, steal, or vandalize. Parents and other family members must set a good example by not bringing things home from the office and by not talking about evading income taxes and the like. Without good parents, good teachers, or law enforcement and judicial personnel with good personal habits, after whom can children model themselves?

Samuel J. Bernardi: Although we do not seem to be able to predict at an early age what child is at risk, we do know that families in our country are breaking down and that there is a high correlation between family breakdown and criminality. Perhaps we should analyze what families are supposed to do and what they are not doing in the hope of developing an effective method of intervention.

Gilman: The problem is even more complex than that. Where there is any kind of family support, most juvenile-court judges will avoid making an adjudication, or, if they make an adjudication, they will not make a disposition or, if they make a disposition, they will not send the child to an institution. Unfortunately, many families do not want or love their children; many parents, for that matter, do not even love themselves or anybody else. They are the debris of a social structure playing havoc with their lives.

Even with all that, the same family that produces the criminal produces the priest, just like in the old movies. From families in torment and from situations of great stress—one-parent families, alcoholism, drug addiction, families struck by war or relocation—often come our creative people, our entertainment figures, and our sports figures, as well as our malignants and our criminals. Eliminating the latter category carries the risk of eliminating as well a very vital component of our country. Perhaps criminality is one of the prices we pay for the kind of society we have. Perhaps the question is whether we need as much criminality as we have. In any event, we cannot lose sight of the fact that very positive benefits flow from conflict.

Note

1. J. Conger and W. Miller, *Personality, Social Class and Delinquency* (New York: Wiley, 1966).

Part II
Biological Influences on Childhood Development

4 The Impact of Neuropsychological Dysfunction on Child Development

David K. Hollingsworth

When originally contacted about the conference on which this book is based, I was asked to recommend anyone to present on the broad topic of the "biological influences of child development" and, specifically, on issues applicable to early-childhood-intervention programming. I gave the organizers a list of persons eminently qualified to do such work. A few months passed, and I received a second phone call. After preparing this chapter, I realize why others had been unwilling to do it. The difficulty lies in the breadth of the concept of "biological predisposers" toward early prosocial behavior.

I have opted in this relatively short space to present the concept of physiologically related disorders that leave a child at risk or more vulnerable to early prosocial behavior. To be more specific, I have chosen to deal with learning disabilities and the biological aspects that are related to learning disabilities in the general frame of their influence on the child's ability, social functioning, and behavior. I hope to convince the reader of the importance of several intervening variables in the process of developing disablement-to-deviance. These variables include the family, schooling, and social maturation. In short, I take the position that although we can train the child for adaptive learning strategies to offset neuropsychological deficits or constitutional deficits, we cannot be successful unless we can "manage" the family, school, and general social environment as well.

I cannot hope to do justice to all the aspects of each theoretical position for each variation of learning disability (LD), which includes specific reading disorders, hyperactivity, attentional and perceptual deficits, and academic-performance deficits. I have decided to use a current case study to exemplify the common etiology of LD and its potential outcomes.

In recent exchanges that I have participated in in special education, early childhood intervention, delinquency, and rehabilitation, biological influences has been a banner concept. I have listened to and delivered papers on topics ranging from LD and brain dysfunction to mental retardation and rehabilitation principles and practices with younger children. The theme that consistently underlies many papers is that LDs lead to a greater proclivity toward early prosocial behavior and later delinquent behavior. The biological roots or etiology of this are cited in both the lay and research literature and range from minimal brain dysfunction to various organic brain syndromes.

This chapter will review some of these major biological theories concerning LDs. More importantly, I will present a case study that is very typical of the processes that we will be concerned with in this book: that is, can we trace the development of early prosocial behavior to a singular biological cause? If we can, can we then also relate it back to larger social outcomes in that child's life?

General Issues

The usual focus of juvenile-delinquency conferences is that delinquency per se is not a psychiatric symptom but a socially ascribed label. A child engages in some sort of socially proscribed behavior that leads to detention and adjudication in the juvenile court. The key to the whole process rests on the social expectations for behavior of children and society's view of so-called deviance for that age group.[1] Usually missing in such discussions are the links between the social process of governing the behavior of youth and the perspective of child mental health. Much of the individual- or person-centered research in delinquency can be divided according to its conceptual focus into genetic (physiological), psychodynamic, or developmental psychological approaches. Biological research has focused largely on two searches: (1) one for a physiological or hereditary predisposition toward delinquency, and (2) one for a biological or neuropsychological mechanism that might predispose a child toward delinquent adaptation.[2]

The constitutional approach has its roots in Lombroso's conception of the criminal as an atavistic throwback[3] and in Sheldon's demonstration of a correlation between mesomorphism and delinquency,[4] a correlation confirmed by the Gluecks in 1979.[5] We know now that this can be explained as much through environmental adaptation as through constitutional tendency. Through the 1960s and 1970s, articles suggested the XYY chromosome's relationship to criminal behavior. Specifically, what has been suggested is that XYY males are more likely to be institutionalized—usually for crimes against property, not against other persons.[6] These males will tend to be less intelligent when compared to XY males as a group. This led Mednick and Christiansen to suggest intelligence, not chromosomal aberration, as the relevant variable.[7] More importantly, Mednick has since postulated that the intervening variable between genetic loading and delinquent behavior is a deficit in response inhibition, itself consequent to low autonomic responsiveness that impairs *social learning.*

Temporal-lobe disorders, psychomotor epilepsy, neuropsychological deficits, trauma to the central nervous system, hyperactivity, and psychomotor deprivation have also been correlated with delinquent behavior and more strongly with prosocial behavior. When these conditions are identified in the child, we must ask whether they reflect an underlying biological predisposition *directly* producing delinquency or whether the independent variable *merely induces* adaptive failure, thus leading to delinquency. In the latter case, we are left with the conclusion that *the inherently limited are inclined toward socially deviant behavior.*

Berman and Siegel similarly observed a high frequency of neuropsychological deficits in a delinquent group when they screened both delinquent and nondelinquent groups.[8] This suggests a theory of etiology in which these youngsters would be predisposed toward adaptive failure and future delinquency: that is, delinquency is consequent to developmental failure in academic mastery. Unfortunately, this has not yet been thoroughly or rigorously confirmed. At any rate, there does seem to be a relationship between neurological deficits and delinquent behavior. Most important, however, is the fact that there are intervening variables in the determination of future delinquent behavior; the child's psychoneurological deficits merely set the initial stage.

I hope to establish that no one conceptual approach is sufficient in itself to explain delinquency. In the broadest sense, delinquency can be conceptualized as a variety of behavioral adaptations of persons reflecting various biological, developmental, psychological, and social variables sharing one thing in common—adaptations that are socially deviant.

The Case of Andy: An Exemplary Example

Let me begin with an example of the conditions that are common in cases in which we can actually identify an etiology or biological root for delinquency. Andy was five and one-half years old when his parents brought him into the clinic for evaluation. Their concern centered on their difficulty in disciplining Andy, intensified by his kindergarten teacher's evaluation that he was easily distracted, inattentive, and hyperactive. The teacher also reported experiencing discipline problems and stated that Andy had a number of visual-motor difficulties suggesting probable perceptual problems.

Andy had been in school for four months prior to his evaluation. He had considerable difficulty in performing tasks most five-year-olds can do quite easily. For example, he could not cut out paper figures and paste them on another sheet. His drawing skills and ability to copy letters and numbers were far below those acceptable for his age level. He could not build objects with blocks. His teacher often tried to help him after he performed poorly on a task, but Andy usually just walked away. Further, he seemed unable to focus his attention on any one activity for a sustained time. He also seemed to run into or often over objects that were in his way. The teacher felt that he should be evaluated and that he might require special placement at school.

Andy had been a full-term baby with no apparent developmental incidents during the mother's pregnancy. His birth was very difficult, however, with the labor lasting well over twenty hours, necessitating the use of forceps. The umbilical cord had become wrapped around his neck, and he was reported as being anoxic. With intensive care and sound medical management, Andy went home with his parents five days later, with no signs of serious complications.

Implications for Child Development

Many of the signs seen at the early age, especially neurological and perceptual signs, are more of a suggestive nature than a precise symptom manifestation. In this case, as in many of the cases that have been used to link delinquency with neuropsychological deficits, precise diagnosis of a minimal brain damage (MBD) label to account for the poor academic performance, suspected LDs, and later delinquency is difficult. Since the symptoms of MBD we can identify at this stage are ambiguous, the phrase is being used as a catchall and is often misused at best.

Many of the commonly accepted indicators of cerebral damage are also found in persons who do not manifest organic pathology. The elusiveness of this issue is indicated by the fact that abnormal electroencephalogram (EEG) patterns are often used as signs of cerebral dysfunction, but generalized abnormal brain activity is also found in children who have long-term behavioral problems. Moreover, prolonged birth labor is not a sure sign of automatic brain damage. L.B. Silver has studied children like Andy extensively and found that the majority do not have abnormal EEG patterns nor do they evidence other significant neurological signs such as abnormal reflexes.[9] It should be added that Silver has also shown that drug therapy lessens the hyperkinesis and distractability of many of these children.

Andy's Development

Andy's pediatrician noted that Andy had shown continual development progress, but at a slower than normal rate. For instance, he was unable to sit without aid until he was nine months old; did not crawl until thirteen months; did not walk until nineteen months; spoke only single words at twenty months. Further, Andy was toilet-trained at thirty-six months but still wet the bed occasionally. Andy fell on his head four times when he was around two—all in a two-month period—and he landed on his brow each time. He did not lose consciousness at any time nor did he have any evidence of concussion (that is, high fever, convulsions, or severe illnesses).

As Andy grew older, his overall development was slower than average but not grossly retarded. He was the first of three children in a white middle-class family. His mother considered him an unplanned pregnancy. Andy's parents had just had a third child—a much-desired girl—ten months prior to his referral. His mother reported that Andy's little brother, eighteen months younger, had almost caught up with Andy developmentally.

Andy's mother said the chief problem is that he will not cooperate with her. He will not follow directions, and spankings and shouting seem to have no effect at all. Andy has frequent temper tantrums characterized by kicking, holding his breath, and screaming. His mother responds by yelling at him to stop and threatening to spank him. He usually ignores her and thus gets the spanking anyway. His mother reported she has become exasperated at his being into everything at once and at his constant running inside and out of the house. She complained of his inability to sustain play activity or to stay in one place for any length of time. The constant litter of toys scattered throughout the house and his refusal to pick up after himself have become a constant source of irritation.

These concerns have become somewhat more noticeable due to increased friction and increased fighting, usually over toys, between Andy and his brother. Andy has resorted to hitting his brother, who consequently runs to the mother. The mother intervenes and reported that she usually lets the younger boy have his way on the assumption Andy is older and should know better. Both boys are punished if they disturb their new sister.

Learning Disabilities: A Biological Perspective of Etiology

At this point, it is important to define some crucial concepts and discuss some of the more recent theoretical contributions about learning theory, at least the biological or neurophysical evidence. Probably the single most immediate reason for a child's referral to a child-psychiatric clinic, child-guidance clinic, or evaluation center is difficulty in school. Unfortunately, as is readily visible in Andy, these children quickly earn an aura and are seen with a tunnel vision caused by their discipline problems. Critically important aspects of their unique learning and behavioral disorders are then often overlooked. It is very important to remember that the child is a physical organism functioning in a social environment in a psychological manner.[10] It is, therefore, very naive to search for a single cause for LDs and behavioral disorders or even for delinquent behavior. Rather, each is caused by any number of factors, all of which can be highly interrelated.

Just what an LD is still needs answering since much of the present confusion concerning LD has resulted from the multiplicity and variation within the definitions. Kirk first used the term *learning disability* to refer to retardation disorders, or developmental delay in one or more of the processes of speech, language, hearing, spelling, writing, or mathematics.[11] He further suggested that the disability stemmed from possible cerebral dysfunction and/or emotional or behavioral disturbances. His use of the term excluded mental retardation, sensory deprivation, and cultural and instructional focus. Bateman extended the definition by describing children with LDs as those who manifest an educationally significant discrepancy between their estimated intellectual performance and their actual performance levels.[12] She also relates LD to a loss of function in the learning processes, which may or may not be accompanied by manifest central nervous system dysfunction. Bateman, like Kirk, excluded generalized mental retardation, educational and cultural deprivation, and severe sensory losses.

More recently, the Education for All Handicapped Children Act of 1975 states that LDs may be manifested in disorders of listening, thinking, reading, writing, spelling, or mathematics.[13] Further, LDs include conditions that have been referred to as perceptual handicaps, brain injuries, MBD, dyslexia, and developmental aphasia. They do not include learning problems due to visual, hearing, or motor handicaps, mental retardation, emotional disturbances, or to environmental disadvantage.

How much of a problem is this? The confusion caused from clinician orientation and definitional clarity has led to very confusing data concerning LDs. Incidence figures have ranged from 3 percent to 20 percent. Evaluations under the Education for All Handicapped Children Act reveal an incidence of about 3 percent.[14] Not surprisingly, that incidence rises to 40 percent within the inner-city schools.

Remarkably, a search of the now-large body of literature of hyperactivity—LDs—childhood mental illness indicates we do not yet fully understand the relationship between the biological, organismic impairments and LDs (or between the neurological impairments and behavioral disorders). We do know that certain physical and psychological factors predispose a child toward learning and behavioral difficulties, but we certainly do not know why. I must stress that environmental conditions have profound effects on even organismic or constitutional factors; unfortunately, the answers to both "how much" and "how so" remain relatively obscure.

Disorders of the Central Nervous System

Golden and Anderson saw several advantages in using the brain-injury theory to account for both LDs and behavioral disorders.[15] The most obvious advantage of the theory—that learning does take place in the brain—allows for explaining LDs (and consequent developmental or maturational lags, hyperkinesis, and behavioral/emotional disturbances) as special cases of brain dysfunction. This offers the possibility of integrating many vastly differing etiological theories, which, in turn, lend themselves to simplification of diagnosis and formulation of innovative rehabilitation planning.

The second advantage in looking at the central nervous system as the source of the LD and behavior disorder is the identification of a single deficit as the cause of a myriad of seemingly unrelated symptoms in the LD child. A common etiology then suggests a common remediation.

Third, there is growing recognition that those properly diagnosed as suffering from MBD have ample rehabilitation possibilities.[16] Thus with accurate data, clinicians can specify *very* individualized remedial programs to maximally develop the child's potential. Finally, evidence has indicated that some LD children are indeed brain injured and that many children with limited brain injuries meet the defining characteristics of learning-disabled.[17]

Biological Evidence Supporting the
Brain-Injury Hypothesis

There are substantial questions concerning the effectiveness of the EEG in diagnosing LDs. EEG will identify only 50 percent of known brain-dysfunction injuries. The Mayo Clinic has shown that up to 15 or 20 percent of the normal population will show abnormal EEG patterns.[18] Therefore, a negative EEG (that is, the lack of any noticeable abnormality) does not necessarily mean an intact brain, only the absence of EEG abnormalities.

Results of EEG research with LD children is important, however. Many studies of EEG patterns of LD children show few, if any, signs of active seizure activity. An overall evaluation of the research suggests the incidence of abnormal EEG patterns in LD populations to be about 60 percent as compared with a 20 percent incidence in control (normal) children. When LD is limited to specific reading disorders, Penn found, the incidence rate rises to 70 to 75 percent as compared with 5 to 10 percent in an applicable control group.[19] Penn also found no difference between children with reading problems resulting from birth and children known to have acquired the deficit through later brain injury.[20]

The second type of medical evidence comes from physical neurological examination, which usually consists of tests of cranial-nerve functions, reflexes, cerebral function, motor and sensory function, and general cerebral function, including emotional responsiveness, memory, social skills, and intelligence. Unfortunately, like the EEG, the neurological examination has serious drawbacks. Primary problems include lack of standardization of the technique, dependence on the experience and skill of the individual physician, and the meaning of soft versus hard signs. "Soft" neurological signs are uncertain indicators, since they occur fairly frequently in persons without any impairment. Unfortunately, the signs associated with LD are limited and are considered soft. Researchers have shown that 90 percent of LD children showed significant soft signs. Only 23 percent of these children also had "hard" signs. Overall, 94 percent of these children had some sort of neurological abnormality. The more frequent soft signs included problems with balance, coordination, and speech. Less frequent were abnormalities in responding to double tactile stimulation, disorders of muscle tone, and indications of overflow movements. Twenty-two percent of these LD children were hyperkinetic.[21]

This longitudinal approach to studying LD children has been replicated several times. Each study generally supports a relationship between LD and brain dysfunction. One noteworthy study (Lucas, Rodin, and Simson)[22] of seventy-two children referred as likely to be LD suggests that children with a history of birth difficulty also showed signs of brain impairment such as abnormal reflexes, a history of walking late, or other neurological problems.[23] These children were also more likely to have had neurological signs and to be hyperactive.[24] Wikler, Dixon, and Parker found that the number of neurological signs seen in LD children was associated with birth weight.[25] These authors suggest that premature babies, who are more susceptible to brain damage, are also more likely to develop LDs.[26]

The third major line of research linking LD to brain injury in children is genetics. These theories argue that many LDs result from biochemical deficiencies in the brain that are a result of hereditary factors. The difficulty of collecting sufficient genetic data has made support for this research very sketchy. McGlannan attempted to study the genetic factors in three generations of sixty-five families, each of which contained at least one child labelled as reading-disordered.[27] All the children scored above ninety on the Weschler Intelligence Scale for Children (WISC). Most exhibited disorders of laterality, maturational lag, inability to perform under stress, finger-indentification problems, and poor motor coordination. He also found a 68 percent rate of twinning in the three generations, which is three times higher than would be expected. The greatest rate of LDs was in siblings of the twins, which suggests these families were more vulnerable to specific LDs.

One major difficulty with this type of study is controlling the interaction between environmental and genetic influences. Even a conservative interpretation of these findings, however, supports a biological predisposition or higher risk of incurring biologically related LDs in a family with a history of hereditary anomalies.

Psychological Evidence Supporting the
Brain-Injury Hypothesis

Psychological tests are very useful in diagnosing limited brain dysfunction that does not show marked motor or sensory deficits. This type of brain injury or dysfunction has most often been theoretically associated with LDs and later delinquency.

The most common approach to neuropsychological assessment in both children and adults involves the level-of-performance method, based on the argument that brain-damaged subjects will do more poorly on psychological tests sensitive to brain injury than control groups of subjects.

The attempt in practice is to set for each test a cutoff value, a score below which represents a nonnormative condition. Commonly used tools are the Bender-Gestalt, Reitan, and Halstead batteries and specific tools of visual-angle perception, right-left (lateralization) confusion, visual recall, naming speed, manual dexterity, and reaction time (to mention only the more prevalent procedures). The major finding of any subset of these test results and research is that there are clearly performance-level signs of organicity in some LD children.

The second group of psychometric data on brain injury and LDs deals with right and left body-side performance. The right cerebral hemisphere of the human brain controls motor functions on the left side of the body, primary auditory input from the left ear, and left-half visual input from both eyes. The left hemisphere does the same for the right body side. These facts provide a powerful method for localizing and identifying cerebral dysfunctions. For example, an injury in the left hemisphere would be likely to impair motor movement or tactile, auditory, or visual input from the right side. By comparing one side of the body with the other, deficits that suggest a cerebral lesion can be identified. The intact side serves as a control, providing performance standards for the other side.

The findings of this research are predictably complex. For instance, a child having sensory and motor symptoms of lateralized cerebral damage will more likely have cognitive deficits. Similarly, the association of motor, sensory, and cognitive losses with LD has been substantiated. This research has been summed up by Golden and Anderson, who found the following for LD children.[28]

First, motor and sensory findings implicating the left hemisphere were accompanied by verbal losses, while motor-sensory findings implicating the right hemisphere were accompanied by nonverbal losses in ten to fourteen-year-old LD children. Second, impairment in left-hemisphere auditory function associated with verbal losses was found in LD children. Third, verbal-impaired LD children had difficulty with left-hemisphere verbal tasks, as expected, but not with right-hemisphere spatial tasks. Finally, 60 percent of LD children had lateralization impairments in either motor or sensory skills, or both. These four findings strongly suggest that the test performance of LD children is very consistent with that of brain-injured children.

In the most powerful method of using psychometric data to evidence brain dysfunction, pattern analysis, the clinician uses a large number of tests to measure some series of independent behaviors and of the function of the brain. This allows for integration of the findings to clearly identify and articulate not only the deficit but the location of that injury or lesion. Using such an approach on forty LD cases, Golden and Anderson found thirty-one cases to have patterns of deficits similar to those found in known brain-injured children.[29]

Andy: The Testing and Diagnostic Findings

The neurological consultation included both an EEG and a physical neurological examination. Andy's EEG was normal for his age. There was no evidence of generalized dysfunction in the brain nor of any abnormality localized in a specific area of the brain (lateralization). Reflex development and motor coordination were below his age level but not grossly abnormal. There was difficulty in fine-motor coordination and perception. The neurologist suggested a preliminary diagnosis of MBD.

The psychological evaluation clearly identified attentional problems, distractibility, a mental age of four years, one month, and problems in fine motor, pattern recognition, and visual recall.

He had a great deal of scatter in the testing (that is, he failed some items that were easy for his age and passed other, more difficult items). Andy did well on vocabulary and verbal concepts but did poorly on subtests requiring perceptual or motor skills. His most striking deficits involved his inability to visualize objects in space and to execute tasks involving fine-motor skills. Andy's gross-motor skills were adequate for his age. He could, therefore, walk and reach adequately but could not, for example, put a small toy-train car on the rails.

Impact of Family Dynamics

Andy's responses to the *Tasks of Emotional Development* (TED) cards revealed expressions of sibling rivalry and worthwhileness because of a perceived lack of ability to do tasks expected of him. He pictured the mother on the cards as always angry and demanding the child to do something that he could not do. These responses led to the observation of Andy with his mother.

Andy and his mother entered the observation room together, and Andy immediately went to explore and enthusiastically began to play with the toys he found. His exclamations were not directed to me or to his mother. When Mrs. B told him to be quiet so she could listen to me, Andy complied but went on playing. His play pattern was very animated and consisted of gross manipulation of the toys for a short period, after which he moved on to the next toy. He did not really play with the toys but only held them and banged them on the table. He really liked the "Boppo" inflated clown but could not hit it unless standing very close to it. Mrs. B's only reaction to Andy was to quiet him when he got a little loud. He responded for awhile, and then the noise volume of his play rose.

When they were given a puzzle to work together, Andy had to be brought over to the table by his mother to work on it. He kept walking away, and his mother did not talk to him after the initial instructions. She finally did the puzzle herself.

It was very evident from this interaction procedure that Mrs. B tended to speak to her son only when he was engaged in disruptive behavior. She made no real effort to teach Andy how to do the tasks and would finish them herself when Andy's attention went somewhere else. She did not encourage his cooperation or reinforce it.

A Discussion of the Biological Implications

Andy's case offers several important findings consistent with a biological root of his LDs (as identified by the teacher) and behavior disorders (as evidenced by the mother). The signs are commonly associated with the syndrome traditionally labeled MBD. First there was the history of difficult labor and birth trauma (anoxia), which are associated with a higher risk of LD later on. Second, there was the visual-perceptual dysfunction that probably caused the early falls that occurred when he was learning to walk. This accident-proneness was probably due to a problem with synthesizing motor-visual data. Further, he also showed an ability to perform well in some tasks but not others, consistent with MBD and LD children.

Unfortunately, children with LDs often get pressure from parents who do not realize the disablement. For instance, Andy's behavior of "not minding" permeated his mother's view of him. He grew more frustrated from the punishment for his inability to finish a task and began to "tune-out." His tantrums were a response to this frustration. Most unfortunately, these became more severe as they lasted, because the child had difficulty controlling or inhibiting the behavior once it began. This is common to brain-damaged children who suffer disinhibition and gradually become wilder and more destructive as they play with some toys and certain games.

Sibling rivalry was probably reinforcing the negative self-concept Andy was forming. School relationships had taken a similar bent. His mother felt Andy was the "least" of her children. Soon, Andy had no choice but to accept this data, as his poor performance in school reinforced it. What else but a continuation and exacerbation of his already deviant response style could occur? He is at the gate of a very self-reinforcing, self-destructive downward spiral. Yes, there is a clear biological basis to this, and the end point would very likely be deviance in the form of juvenile delinquency. But there remains the question of how one intervenes to halt this at the very minimum and, at the maximum, begin rehabilitative and remedial training.

Intervention and Implications

Andy is not an uncommon example of the children referred as probable LD to many clinics. What is uncommon is the potential for the reversal of negative outcomes of this case. After explaining the results to Andy's parents and discussing the etiology of his problems specifically, we suggested strategies to the family to help overcome a few of the most prominent problems.

The parents and teachers needed to know that Andy's difficulty with visual-motor skills (eye-hand coordination) meant problems in fine-motor coordination but an inability to learn in regular schooling. Also, the parents would need help to recognize behaviors that resulted from neuropsychological impairment and not to expect him to be capable of doing all things.

Andy was recommended for an LD class in the first grade so as to get early special education geared to his special needs. Further, Andy and his mother were recommended for participation in filial therapy (involving mother in play therapy with her child). The mother is taught to accept the child's expressions and reflect their feelings to build trust for both in each other. Filial therapy has proven to be very effective for parents who have difficulty in expressing positive emotions and simply communicating with their children.

Mrs. B learned how to deal with Andy's hyperactivity through behavior-modification techniques. This was added for her and other mothers of MBD children to ensure the modification of the child's behavior through the use of rewards and social approval for less active behavior. Within twelve months, the overall results were very consistent and loving child-mother interactions. In fact, many of Andy's behavior problems were completely extinguished, and he was performing very well in his LD class.

The use of filial and behavioral-therapy principles with the mother led to a home environment in which expectations and standards of behavior were clearly defined and realistic. Structuring Andy's educational environment to compensate for his perceptual difficulties led to excellent academic progress. All of this led to frequent praise for his successes, which fed his feelings of mastery and self-image as a worthwhile person.

Each child with similar but not identical disorders would respond differently. We are particularly prone of late to describe children in terms of "intellectual potential," and estimate of a child's upper limit of ability. This case presentation affirms, however, one's natural belief that none of us can determine with any certainty what that can be. Parents and school personnel must deal directly with the intellectual and behavioral disabilities these children face. It is *not* an easy or often overtly rewarding process. It is possible, however, to salvage children with neurological LDs and to give them the opportunity to reach greater levels of development and self-sufficiency than ever thought possible.

Conclusions and Comments

The question now is not so much whether there are biological influences that result in physical behaviors, but rather how important this distinction is. I conclude that brain injury or, more generally, biological deficits are no more of one kind than most children are. Many variables must be taken into account in order to understand the relationship between biological deficits and the child's behavior.

Location of the Damage

Just where the damage is will strongly affect the outcomes. Some injuries will result in visual deficits, others in verbal deficits, and still others in motor losses. Some injuries will result in profound deficits in one or more of these areas, while others will have no observable effects. The treatment intervention must acknowledge that the child's behavior is formed most by the environmental influences interacting with the child's specific conditions.

Extent of Damage

The larger the area affected, the greater the number of deficits and the more pernicious the deficits. Also, the larger the injury, the more likely there will be behavioral effects associated. Finally, the greater the damage, the more likely mental retardation will be associated and the less likely the child will have very much potential for normative life. This does not suggest an incapacity, but merely more needs that require special resolution.

Causes

Each disorder produces demonstrably different results in the child's behavior. The specific neurological processes obviated will vary both in terms of severity and specificity from child to child. Specific attention must be paid to strengths and deficits of the child's environment and how those interface with the child's special conditions.

Age of the Child and Time of Injury

The development and age of each child must be considered. Since a three-year-old does not face the same environmental demands as does a nine-year-old, specific deficits often do not become problems until the child's environs change. Also, if the injury is not attributable to neonatal or birth trauma, the age of onset is critical. Those brain injuries that occur postlanguage development make life easier for the child than do those that occur prior to twenty-four months of age.

Complexity of the Child's Environmental Demands

The management of the environment makes programming work, whether we are discussing MBD, LDs, delinquency, or profound mental retardation. The amount, specificity, and time of damage to the child's central nervous system are crucial variables in predicting the outcome for that child. These are a far second, however, to the social environment, and particularly, to the home environment of that child. As Andy's case demonstrates, the social and human services technologies are very sophisticated and, when applied, can have marked impact.

The real issues then become how to determine (and anticipate) what environmental characteristics the child needs to face in maturing, and how to structure that development to provide opportunities for successful adaptation, rather than adaptive failure that increases the risk that the child will later exhibit prosocial behavior and delinquency.

Notes

1. D. Zinn, "Therapeutic and Preventive Intervention in Juvenile Delinquency," in *Treatment of Emotional Disorders in Children and Adolescents,* eds. G.P. Sholevar, R.M. Benson, and B.J. Blinder (New York: Spectrum Publications, 1980).

2. Ibid.

3. S. Glueck and E. Glueck, *Toward a Typology of Juvenile Offenders* (New York: Grune & Stratton, 1970).

4. W. Sheldon, *Varieties of Delinquent Youth* (New York: Harper, 1949).

5. S. Glueck and E. Glueck, *supra*, note 3.

6. S. Kessler and R.H. Moos, "The XYY Karyotype and Criminality: A Review," *Journal of Psychiatric Research* 7 (1970): 153-170.

7. S.A. Mednick and K.O. Christiansen, *Biosocial Basis of Criminal Behavior* (New York: Halstead, 1977).

8. A. Berman and A. Siegel, "A Neuropsychological Approach to Etiology, Prevention and Treatment of Juvenile Delinquency," in *Child Personality and Psychopathology: Current Topics,* ed. A. Davis (New York: Wiley, 1976).

9. A. Berman and A. Siegel, *supra*, note 8.

10. J. Abrams, "Learning Disabilities," in *Treatment of Emotional Disorders in Children and Adolescents,* eds. G.P. Sholevar, R.M. Benson, and B.J. Blinder (New York: Spectrum Publications, 1980).

11. S.A. Kirk, *Educating Exceptional Children* (Boston: Houghton Mifflin, 1962).

12. B. Bateman, "An Educator's View of a Diagnostic Approach to Learning Disorders," in *Learning Disorders,* vol. 1, ed. J. Hellmuth (Seattle: Special Child Publications, 1965).

13. The Education for All Handicapped Children Act of 1975, 24 U.S.C. §§ 1401-1461 (1976).

14. J. Abrams, *supra*, note 10.

15. S. Golden and S. Anderson, *Learning Disabilities and Brain Dysfunction: An Introduction for Educators and Parents* (Springfield, Ill.: Thomas, 1979).

16. R. Gardener, "Minimal Brain Dysfunction," in *Child Development in Normality and Psychopathology,* ed. J.R. Bemporad (New York: Brunner/Mazel, 1980).

17. S. Golden and S. Anderson, *supra*, note 15.

18. R. Gardener, *supra*, note 16.

19. N. Goddes, "The Neuropsychology of Reading Disorders: Parts I & II," *Journal of Learning Disabilities* 11, no. 9 (1978):44-48; 11, no. 10 (1978):37-44.

20. S. Golden and S. Anderson, *supra,* note 15, chaps. 2, 3.

21. Ibid.

22. Ibid.

23. Ibid.

24. Ibid.

25. Ibid.

26. Ibid.
27. Ibid.
28. S. Golden and S. Anderson, *supra,* note 15, chap. 1.
29. S. Golden and S. Anderson, *supra,* note 15.

Commentary

Mary Hughes

We in the March of Dimes have been in the prevention business for some forty years. We would never have beaten polio, however, if we had taken the route that we are discussing today, a very reflective one. Moreover, we could not have solved the polio problem today, in any event, because lawyers would never have let us perform those field tests.

The two special points I would like to make involve the prevention not of crime but of birth defects. Dr. Hollingsworth tried to lay a basis for a biological cause to deviant behavior. Although no one will submit that all such behavior is biologically induced, Hollingsworth did posit some relationship between deviant behavior and learning disability (LD), minimal brain damage (MBD), or birth defect.

Most birth defects, research tells us, are preventable, and, indeed, the United States itself has been successful in the prevention of birth defects. Our infant mortality and our infant morbidity rates were better last year.

This has resulted in part from education. More women today receive prenatal education. More pregnant women today stop smoking. More pregnant women today stop drinking. More pregnant women today practice good nutrition. Why? Because today there are good prevention programs and good educational programs available.

Many of the eleven- to fourteen-year-olds who become pregnant manifest learning disabilities. This is the group that drops out of school or that is in special-education classes. This group has the poorest physical health habits. This group has more obesity, less physical fitness, and more truancy. This group can perhaps be compared to other youngsters who are quite difficult to work with and in whom any type of behavioral change does not come easy.

Research at the University of Rochester has found that most pregnant adolescents between the ages of eleven and fourteen do not really enjoy sexual intercourse at that age but find it difficult to say "no."[1] For the last four years, we have conducted an aggressiveness training program for these young women, which teaches that "It's O.K. to say 'no way'." The indications are that this educational approach, although not 100 percent successful, is effective.

We have also conducted smoking-cessation programs, using the Harvard Smoking Cessation Model, which is based on classical behavior modification, and have been getting results on drinking cessation, also. This success has come despite the fact that teaching high-school girls is extremely difficult.

An eight-year study of Catholic education, released recently, demonstrated through standardized test scores that students in Catholic schools performed better in four content areas, including reading and math, than their public-school counterparts. The children involved attributed their better performance to an understanding of the environment, an understanding of the standards, and knowledge that the standards would be enforced. Interestingly, these children felt that the discipline they received was fair; in similar interviews, in public schools, where presumably discipline was not as rigid, the children indicated they did not understand what the discipline was and thought it unfair. People perform better, therefore, when they understand the expectations.

In terms of early childhood intervention, we have today a whole new field of perinatology. Intensive care units are now able to do things that were impossible just five years ago. The social and behavioral research with regard to infant stimulation and the like that has come out of intensive care units is astounding. The real difficulty is that children leaving the intensive care unit are almost lost until some other system picks them up again at the age of five.

Note

1. M. Zelnick, "Sexual Activity Among Adolescents," in *Pregnancy and Childbearing During Adolescence: Research Priorities for the 1980s,* eds. E. McAnarney and G. Stickle (March of Dimes Birth Defects Foundation Publication) (New York: Allen R. Liss, 1981), p. 34.

Roundtable

Scott: We think of these young ladies getting pregnant between the ages of eleven and fourteen as delinquent; they are not "supposed" to get pregnant or even to have sex. Should we intervene before the pregnancy?

Hughes: We *must* intervene before the pregnancy. Such pregnancies produce seven times more damaged babies than do pregnancies in women between the ages of nineteen and twenty-four. Young girls, particularly young girls in precarious situations, need aggressiveness training. These young girls have never role played and have never had the type of counseling they need.

Scott: Apparently many mothers are negligent in providing their daughters with assertiveness or aggressiveness training. No matter how close she is to her parents, no girl is likely to tell her mother that she is beginning to have sexual relations. Given that situation we must deal with the whole cohort rather than wait for behavior manifesting a child at risk. They are all at risk.

Steele: We must increase the use by the pediatrics profession of screening tests and other devices that can determine children already in difficulty. So many signs, whether minimal brain damage (MBD) or hyperactivity or whatever, are discernible in the second or third year, if not earlier.

This does not mean one is predicting delinquency but rather discovering children who are at risk for problems. Their cognitive, emotional, and social development may or may not include delinquency. These children can be discovered earlier through birth defects. Regardless of what else happens, a bad start in life lays the groundwork for later problems.

Bahlmann: Although we are focusing on intervention as a mechanism for preventing future delinquency, such intervention can in fact prevent a whole myriad of problems, including future physical deprivation. We may be protecting society from further child abuse, from further physical problems, birth defects, problem mothers, and the like.

Hollingsworth: Conservatively, about half of the children with learning disabilities turn out to have brushes with the law. A person who consistently experiences failure learns adaptive ways of responding and of acquiring the needed recognition. Moreover, what likely occurs is that the child having few avenues open to him uses the ones that are open, which oftentimes involve delinquent behavior.

Hughes: Much of the progress in the biological and physical realm is related to government support. The W.I.C. (Women, Infants and Children) Program, a food-supplement program, has significantly improved maternal nutrition, which is closely correlated with prevention of low birth weight or premature babies. Unfortunately, programs such as the pregnancy program in the Department of Health and Human Services may be in jeopardy.

Bahlmann: Dr. Hughes, does the kind of education of young girls you refer to fall within your definition of sex education?

Hughes: Yes. Unfortunately, as soon as one says "sex education," everybody becomes angry and fears that such education causes promiscuity. Schools cannot provide sex education by themselves, but they, along with families and churches, do have an important role.

Richard S. Eynon: When do the experts feel it is necessary to take that child from the fourteen-year-old mother who is learning disabled (LD) or whatever? In any event, when does one take away the second child of that same mother, who is now sixteen? Is there ever a time when that is good preventive medicine? Most constitutional law involves the balancing of interests; does there not come a time when the individuality of the child is superior to the rights of the mother?

Scott: Why do you want to take the child from its mother? There is an assumption that those girls are out on their own and not living at home with their own mothers. Most of these girls live at home, along with all the other children, and the new baby is brought up almost like a sister to the young girl. In my city, the public schools are trying to make these young girls good mothers through child development, health, nutrition, and other classes that their own mothers didn't get. Rather than take the child from these young mothers, therefore, we should support these young mothers so that child neglect, child abuse, and other evils can be avoided.

Gilman: Generally speaking, the newborn should not be taken from the mother. Research involving children from terrible natural family situations who are put into either preadoptive homes or institutions demonstrates that those alternatives to the natural family are worse or no better than the natural family. Children taken from families because of abuse are, in turn, abused in institutions or foster families. Unfortunately, many of the prevention programs have focused on removing the child, helping the child to adapt, or helping the foster family to work with the child rather than providing the fundamental support necessary for the natural family, even though the mother may have LD, or even though there may be retardation or economic and social pressures. Most of the intervention is not geared toward making the natural family situation a better one.

Bahlmann: One Lilly Endowment Project in Indianapolis tries to deal with the child's environment by working with the mother and the child. Dr. Hollingsworth, what is the reaction of the parent when a problem is diagnosed as having a biological cause?

Hollingsworth: More often than not, the parent feels a certain amount of guilt, which requires time to subside. Indeed, probably our first intervention is to help the parent past that stage. The diagnosis or the label is ultimately a minor barrier for the parents.

Steele: Parents do not distinguish between biological or environmental problems. The parent is interested in whether this is a good kid or a deviant one. The abuse and neglect occur when the parents view the child as somewhat unsavory to the parents' own goals, which could occur with a birth defect, prematurity, sexual behavior, or anything else. Many parents are able to empathize with the child and do not get upset by a birth defect or prematurity. They adapt to the child and do a beautiful job of child rearing. On the other hand, a child born to parents whose own necessity is to have a child that is "perfect" is in trouble.

Bahlmann: I have on a number of occasions heard parents say, "Thank God it's physical. I thought it was my fault." Is the medical or psychological state of the art advanced enough currently to justify mandatory testing of children at very young ages?

Conrad: A few years ago, I visited an institution in Maine for unusually difficult children. They showed me a boy rejected by his parents, by various state schools in the state of Oregon, and by numerous foster homes and other institutions. The state of Oregon, desperate about the situation, had made inquiries among seventy-five different child-caring agencies that seemed interested or capable of handling such situations. Only two indicated an interest in taking this boy, one of them the Maine institution.

The situation, as I gathered it from interviews with the boy and physicians there, was a relatively simple psychopharmacology one: With proper use of the appropriate drug, an apparently uncontrollable situation could be brought under control. I bring this up because the current state of the art for the very difficult child is close to abysmal, and such situations are often exploited by quacks and frauds.

A most urgent research topic involves what can be done for these enormously difficult children who come from every class of society—not just the poor—but for whom no really adequate services are available anywhere.

Schweinhart: I am puzzled by all the concern about compulsory programs. We should provide programs so attractive that compulsoriness is not a problem. We should not be so concerned about constraining an individual's choice with regard to joining programs they do not find attractive in any event.

Steele: I agree. Most parents are very interested in their child's development and, more specifically, whether he is doing as well as the kid down the street. They are delighted to find ways to check that development. Mandatoriness will not help. A person who dislikes a particular testing program will not bring his children to it even if it is mandatory.

Part III
Environmental Influence on Childhood Development

5

Delinquent Youth in the Obsolete Environment

John P. Conrad

In a brilliant lecture delivered in January 1973 at the Phillips Academy in Andover, Massachusetts, Professor Daniel P. Moynihan (then ambassador to India, now senator from New York) sketched the impact of demographic trends on the structure and the future of American society.[1] The facts were familiar then and are still relevant to the problem we are considering here—the environmental influences that turn too many young people into serious delinquents.

Most of Professor Moynihan's predictions, which I review here as a backdrop to an understanding of our persisting problem of youth delinquency, have proved correct. Moynihan noted that wholly apart from the tragic events of the sixties, that decade was a unique period in American history, and, indeed, in the history of the world. The distinguishing feature in the demography of those times was the baby boom of the fifties, which had evolved into a youth explosion. It was, Moynihan said, "a profound demographic change . . . a one-time change, a growth in population vaster than any that had ever occurred before, or any that will ever occur again, with respect to a particular sub-group in the population—namely those persons from 14 to 24 years of age."[2]

The dimensions of that change must be stated to be appreciated, although surely everyone has a general idea of what happened. Moynihan, reviewing the demographic history of the nation, noted that the size of this subgroup grew, from 1890 to 1960:

> ten percent, eight percent, sometimes not at all. . . . In the whole of that seventy years, the total increase in the population of that age group . . . was 12.5 million persons. Then in the 1960's it grew by 13.8 million persons, an increase of 52 percent in one decade, five times the average rate of the preceding 70 years. it grew by 13.8 million persons; it will grow by 600,000 in the 70's; it will decline in the 1980's. It's all over; it happened once, it will not happen again . . . we shall see an eight percent decline in the 1980's.[3]

Senator Moynihan predicted that the 1980s would be a decade of domestic peace. The title of his lecture was "Peace—." What has happened?

Although we are not fighting a war in a distant country, we can hardly claim to be a nation enjoying domestic peace. There may have been a subsidence of crime and delinquency in the early seventies. It is hard to tell from the Uniform Crime Reports. The numbers of reporting agencies varied so much during this period that we cannot make much sense out of the trends and are at least entitled to the conjecture that the changes in the rates of youth crime did not amount to much. Similarly, if we examine the rate of violent crime in Indianapolis for the nine years from 1970-1978, we find a low of 272.4 per 100,000 in 1973 and a high of 527.4 in 1975, with a rate of 463.7 in 1978. However that may have been during the last two or three years, a resurgence of violent crime has alarmed the public, caused a wave of punitive legislation in the urbanized states, and increased the prison population very considerably, in comparison with a declining population in confinement during the early seventies.

This book is not the place for a full recapitulation of the data or even for making certain that the popular impressions of crime bear any correspondence to reality. The situation is serious, and lawyers and criminologists will do well not to persist in attempts to minimize it. A recent *Newsweek* poll shows that 75 percent of the respondents believe that criminals are more violent than they were five years ago and that 58 percent think that there is more crime in their area than there was a year ago. The majority of those polled were taking precautions against mugging and assault.[4] It is not for you or me to point out that other years may have been as bad or even worse. Our task as professionals in criminal justice is to consider what can be done to relieve a situation generally believed to be intolerable and probably getting worse. As policy scientists, we shall certainly be ignored if we fail in our obligation to suggest social, economic, and legislative changes that might remedy our predicament. We shall not capture much attention by asserting that nothing can be done but to await the coming decline in the youth population.

To arrive at some strategies for relief, I shall skip rapidly and a little dogmatically over issues that would detain a proper scholar for the writing of whole books. The risk that I shall seem to be stating the obvious without illuminating cannot be avoided in the space available here.

The Youth Culture

The most significant effect of the population explosion that Moynihan described was the creation of a youth culture. The shift toward youth in the center of gravity of our population led to a predominance of the values that appealed to youth, unconstrained by fears of the future or the traditions passed on from earlier generations by their parents and the schools they attended.

In his lecture, Moynihan referred to the youth of the sixties as a new social class, "fundamentally isolated from the rest of society. It was isolated on campuses, it was isolated in slums, it was isolated in a way in the armed forces,"[5] which occupied so many during this period and well into the seventies. During that decade, the number of males between the ages of sixteen and nineteen increased by 44 percent, but the number of these young men who were employed increased by only 11 percent. Unemployment was the prevailing condition for those young people who were not drafted for military service.

The youth of the sixties created a new culture: a music, a literature, a style of life, and an attitude toward self and its "actualization" (to use Abraham Maslow's popular, if not clearly intelligible, term) that constituted a culture radically different from what had ever before existed in this country. Attitudes toward old values were skeptical if not negative. The essential question was, "Why not?" Why not do something that was discouraged as unwise or proscribed as immoral by earlier generations? The unacceptable answer was that religion, morals, the laws, or traditional values ran counter to what one wanted to do. Having observed this "strange" generation as a parent, as a professor, and as an administrator of correctional programs, I cannot say that this questioning, abrasive process was entirely bad. This youth revolution accomplished the dissolution of much that was meretricious, hypocritical, or nonsense in our system of values.

It also left us two still powerfully significant effects for the quality and prevalence of delinquency in our times. First, a whole generation came to accept dependency as a tolerable condition of life. Where parents could afford it, young people depended on families for support far beyond the time that had been customary for emancipation in earlier years. Those who were on their own found it quite possible to be "on the government" in one way or another without troubling conscience or pride. This was a whole generation with a lot of time on its hands, which led to another factor significant for the spread of delinquency—the precedence given to personal gratification over other motivations. It was a hedonist culture, and it should have been expected that narcotics and other psychoactive drugs would be widely accepted as natural means for self-gratification. It turned out that although the laws were explicit and strict, and their enforcement was a high priority for the "establishment," the youth culture had little difficulty in evading the antidrug laws, and thereby arrived at a system of values incompatible with obedience to the laws of the land.

I have used a broad brush in this account of a culture to which I had no allegiance. It needs to be said that most of the young people who attained the heights of selfish hedonism tired of the view and descended to the workaday lives that most citizens share. Jerry Rubin's metamorphosis from hippie to stockbroker was the most spectacular such transition, but there were millions who made the retreat from self-realization to more productive lives in less-notable fashion. Nevertheless, the selfishness inherent in this culture was consistent with the callous criminal behavior that has been so evident ever since. This sinister strain in the youth culture began early in families that were ill-equipped to check it. It persisted far into adulthood.

"It's over . . . ,"[6] Senator Moynihan said. In the statistical, demographic sense, he was right. But cultural values, once spread through so large a sector of the population, do not disappear with the aging of the generation in which they were diffused. Values change gradually, affected by social and economic realities confronting the new generation. The youth of the eighties will constitute a much smaller fraction of our population than did the youth of the sixties and seventies, but they are affected by the culture of their predecessors and by new realities resulting in a new youth culture. The outlines of the youth culture of the future can be seen roughly and uncertainly, and it would be rash to attempt sharp predictions. Still, many of the realities that will exert an impact on delinquency are clear enough.

The New Social Realities

Let us begin with the family and the changes that made it less effective as a socializing influence. The nature of the family's socializing function is partly determined by the reasons that caused the child's parents to bring him into the world in the first place. Isaac's ancient injunction to Jacob, "Be fruitful and multiply," was enough for those pastoral times and for many succeeding millennia. The land had to be subdued and the earth replenished. For our forefathers, it was an absolute necessity to produce children—and many of them. Their labor was needed; we know from watching present-day peasant societies how valuable the work of even a small child can be. Later in life, when fathers and mothers became patriarchs and matriarchs, they could count on their progeny to sustain them. Children were the security of their parents, even in industrialized societies, until far into the twentieth century.

That is over, too, at least in the United States. For whatever reason a husband and wife decide to become progenitors, it is not with the expectation that the sacrifices made in youth will be offset by support in old age nor that the work of the contemporary child will have much economic value. For the middle classes, children are an expensive commitment to the future; for the less comfortable classes, the costs may be much less, if not insignificant. But whatever psychological purposes children may serve, their economic value is nil.

Throughout most of history until the recent past, the child was disciplined by the religious beliefs of his parents, by the standards of behavior of tne community in which he was raised, and, perhaps most significantly of all, by the work he did in early life. In peasant societies, the work he did called for the strength he was gradually gaining but no other preparation. Later, as society became more complex, the child was a child and unready for adult life until he had completed a course of education that lengthened as the generations went by, and skills had to be added to strength. The child was a worker, or he was preparing for a career of work for which he was unready until his education was pronounced complete.

That is over too, for many (perhaps for most) children. The child is no longer a worker, nor is his education directed toward a working career. More than anything else, he is a consumer. If his parents are rich, he will sense that he is "entitled," to use the expressive term chosen by Robert Coles, to good things and a privileged place in society. He is still primarily a consumer. At a lesser economic scale, the child still knows that in the secure middle class he can get most of the things he wants with little effort. If he comes from a family on welfare, he will know that like his parents and like most of the adults in his world, he is redundant as far as the legitimate economy is concerned. It will be foolish for him to try, through the system that has no use for him, to get what nobody around him succeeds in getting—regardless of what he hears on television, in school, or elsewhere. The family of such a boy or girl can do little for their offspring except to pass on such wisdom as may have been accumulated about staying out of trouble. The wonder is that some young people who grow up in such circumstances still try to better themselves through the system. It is not a myth that when the word goes around the ghetto that a big company is hiring young people, the line will begin in the small hours of the morning with hundreds seeking work that only dozens will get. The children of the underclass, like their more fortunate peers, are still consumers, but they rely on their wits rather than their parents to get what they would like to consume.

Most children eventually lead productive lives, and most children of the underclass eventually find their ways into some kind of irregular work. For the present, they are expected to do no more than prepare for adulthood by attending school. The future is more ominous. This is no longer an expanding economy, and it will be many years—if ever—before this country enjoys a period of growth such as it did in the fifties and sixties. There will be less room for everyone in a static economy. The upwardly mobile will move up at slower speeds, and the good fortune that some young people enjoy in the lower end of the class structure will befall them less frequently. The prospects are the dimmest of all for the children of the underclass, some of whom will later become the most troublesome delinquents, our most dangerous criminals. They will continue to consume, and their plight will receive little sympathy from those who are more secure but still in straitened circumstances. Such young people have little to lose by choosing to commit criminal acts, and, with no great amount of luck, they have something to gain. Not only can they gain what they need to continue as consumers, but they can also express their resentment of the fortunate.

We can see the results of this perception of the world in the inner-city schools of most of our metropolises. The disorders, the intimidation of other children, the attacks on teachers, and the sheer terrorism that sometimes occurs all tell us that these schools are more like ill-equipped and inappropriately staffed prisons than educational institutions. These children are merely kept off the streets; there are no skills to learn in school that they will need to survive in the world that has no use for them.

As they get older, children derive most of their values from their peers—a process particularly evident during the period of the youth explosion that I have been discussing. Parents have less influence on them, and Moynihan noted that in the times of which he spoke, the subgroup of youth was especially isolated from both their elders and from those who were younger. It was in the solidarity of the groups to which they belonged that the most powerful determinants of conduct could be found. That was so when I was young, and it continues to be true.

The young work out their own typologies. There are *straights*, who are subdivided into brains and jocks; these are young people with talents who are willing to subject themselves to disciplines of study or training so that they can maximize their expectations. Then there are *cools*, who know that they cannot compete successfully with straights in school or in athletics but are well enough provided so that they can relax and consume until another phase of their lives can begin. Finally, there are *rowdies*, who see that conformity to standard behavior is pointless and that the future will be as empty as the present. If the monotony of redundancy is to be relieved, they must create the action—by reckless use of motorcycles and automobiles, by vandalism, and by overt criminal activity, often of a violent nature. In some large cities those from ethnic minorities will form well-organized gangs and discover in them the loyalty and the satisfactions of organized predation.

Nothing in real life is as neat as a typology, but we do not have to peer far into the future to see what will become of the kids who identify with each of these styles of living, nor are any special powers needed to account for them. The cools tend to use narcotics; ethnographers tell us that one need not use dope to be considered cool, but not many cools abstain.[7] Some will drift away from the delinquencies implicit in the use of drugs and into conventional, if not very exciting, lives. Some will become delinquent beyond their engagement in the narcotics traffic. If conventional opportunities are sufficient in number, it is reasonable to expect that most cools will drift out of delinquency.

The rowdies—mostly young people from the underclass, though by no means are all members of the underclass rowdies—constitute the most likely prospects for serious crime and delinquency. They will be arrested more often, and more of them will wind their ways through the courts and into various correctional programs. Again, some of them will be intimidated sufficiently to abstain from serious delinquency, whereas others will drift defiantly into further delinquencies. Opportunity and purposeful intervention by social and criminal-justice agencies will determine how many continue in criminal activity.

When there was a conspicuous class of the idle rich, ennui was its affliction. There was little public concern; after all, there were not enough rich people to inspire great concern about their troubles. Now we have a class of the impoverished and idle young, who punctuate the days of tedium with "action." Too often, the action is destructive and potentially lethal. There are so many of the impoverished young that we have good cause to worry about what they will do in the name of action. We can be certain that if they cannot find action allowed and encouraged by the system, they will not hesitate to choose action that is unacceptable—even intolerable—to the rest of us.

The need for action is easily misunderstood in the sanctuaries of academia. In a book that was popular with policymakers of the Nixon Administration, Edward Banfield made a characteristic statement of the problem that was accurate enough in the statement of the facts but superficial in the discussion of their significance. He observed that the most salient feature of lower-class life is its so-called present-orientation, by which he meant the inability of lower-class persons to plan for or even to consider the future. One of the most important consequences of the present-orientation is the disposition of those so oriented to seek action, leading to "risk-taking, conquest, fighting, and 'smartness' [that] makes lower-class life extraordinarily violent."[8] Banfield implied that members of the lower class are present-oriented because of innate qualities derived from the peasant cultures from which they came. This led him to view their condition as hopeless except that, because of their improvidence, they do not reproduce themselves. Banfield was unable to see that the conditions of life that chronic poverty and unemployment impose on the underclass are much more plausible foundations for improvidence. Life in the redundant classes is tedious, humiliating, and emasculating. If manhood cannot be demonstrated by achievement, is must be sought in action.

Banfield's notions about action and the underclass seem typical of a strain of thought in our neoconservative social philosophies that leads to the dismissal of social problems as inherently insoluble. It is thought futile to attempt to change the underclass because people "like that" are unchangeable. Rather, we should make the crimes to which underclass youth are inclined as difficult to commit as can be arranged; if we cannot change criminals, we can at least "harden" their targets. Without deprecating the desirability of target-hardening, I suggest that the strategy of simple neglect of the underclass problem as an insoluble contradiction to the national commitment to equality and fairness can only lead to increased disorder, violence, and crime. Partial solutions are better than none; effort, whether successful or not, is more compatible with American ideals than surrender to impotence and indifference.

Criminal Justice and the Delinquent Child

Chicago was the birthplace of juvenile justice, and Hull House, the settlement on the West Side founded by Jane Addams, was its cradle. As Miss Addams and her followers saw it, society had to differentiate juvenile delinquency—a problem with a simple logic—from adult criminality. Children who violated the law were in a special kind of trouble because of social handicaps and influences that led to delinquent acts. The utilitarianism that Jane Addams represented readily connected juvenile misbehavior with deprivation, association with adult criminals, lack of parental guidance, and a variety of other destructive influences. The proper strategy for dealing with delinquents, therefore, was not to punish the child in trouble with the law but rather to prevent him from becoming an offender. Hence the juvenile court, and hence, too, a whole catalogue of status offenses: truancy from school, runaways from home, sexual promiscuity, drinking, bad associations, and incorrigibility. Status offenses gave the state a license to intervene like a good parent so that more serious troubles might be averted.

Over time, this approach to justice for the children and protection for the community has worn thin, as we all know. From nearly all liberal quarters, the intervention by the court in the lives of children who have committed no crimes has been seen as indefensibly unjust, and the structure of juvenile justice has been modified accordingly. Treatment of the potential delinquent is a responsibility of which the juvenile court, in the course of this overhaul and in the interests of justice, may be relieved.

In the same interests, but at the other end of the continuum of delinquency, is a pronounced trend away from the positivism and the individualization of the serious juvenile offender. In many states, laws have been enacted to diminish the jurisdiction of the juvenile court over violent juvenile offenders by lowering the maximum age of juvenile status. It is beside the point to debate whether it is wise or efficacious to remove from juvenile court jurisdiction violent juveniles as young as thirteen or fourteen. The point is that this trend expresses the mood of many Americans. It represents an emphasis on retribution—a first priority on the deterrence of delinquency—especially the violent delinquency that characterizes the behavior of underclass youth.

The systems of adult and juvenile justice are prominent—perhaps the most prominent—features of the environment of the delinquent youth. A special feature of both adult and juvenile justice has been unpredictability. Neither an adult nor a juvenile in trouble could be sure what the law meant. Even in the best of times and in the best of courts, the best interest of the child might be seen to be treatment in the community, regardless of the seriousness of his offense. With the erosion of the system because of the immense amount of traffic through the juvenile court, decisions about treatment might be too casually taken and based on assumptions that services would be provided that were actually unavailable. Nominal consequences would ensue from the commission of grave felonies by juveniles; the unpredictable system must have encouraged many youths to persevere in their delinquencies because of the fairly clear message that even if they were caught, serious consequences were unlikely. Few juvenile offenders in any state are committed to residential control. Even when imposed, confinement is likely to be brief, except in a few states in which severe punishments have been introduced for those who commit homicide or other particularly vicious crimes of violence. The juvenile-justice system is not now a serious deterrent to delinquency or a satisfactory corrective to those who engage in it. A distinguished leader in juvenile justice once remarked that the best action with respect to most delinquents is no action at all. This is how the situation now stands, and we do not see a substantial effect on the incidence of juvenile crime.

What Can Be Done?

No "invisible hand" will spontaneously sweep aside the nation's current problems of delinquency. Even though the youth of the sixties and the seventies will soon approach middle age, the diminished number of their successors is ample to match the volume of delinquency experienced in the expansive years of the youth explosion. The underclass, from which the most alarming young delinquents come, will continue to produce babies at rates that exceed the birth rates of the more comfortable classes. At the same time, in the static economy that is to be foreseen, there will be less room for the young. If the present trends continue, we will still have a youth culture of consumers, consuming less than they did in former years and faced with redundancy as far into the future as anyone can see. There is no apparent reason to suppose that the declining influence of the family and the church will be reversed and that the future orientation—so prized by conservative social philosophers like Professor Banfield—will once again be ascendant. Is there any reason to suppose that children of the inner city, served by the same public schools, will be better served in the future than they are now? It is likely that these schools will continue to be more custodial than educational and that support for innovation will be even less available than it has been.

The improbable may happen. The decline in the youth population may be closely followed by an equal decline in the delinquency rate. If so, we may thank the kindly gods of demography, but such trends have never before been so neat; we should not count on such good fortune. We should consider changes in our institutional structures that would turn the youth culture toward different channels of development. What I suggest—though audacious in some respects—is hardly more than a beginning, and I am the first to concede that although I think I know what should be done—at least in part— I do not know how to do it.

First, we must find ways of providing that nurture that working parents cannot. Critics of Aid to Families with Dependent Children (AFDC) programs urge that mothers of children past the age of two should go to work. Maybe they should, just as their more affluent working sisters do. But if working mothers are to be the rule and not the exception, we need a more reliable resource for the care of their children than a willing grandmother, neighbor, or friend down the street. Children shifted around from one caretaker to another and children left mostly to their own devices from an early age are surely not getting the support for standards of conduct and the stability of expectations that they require.

Accordingly, I propose active encouragement of responsible centers for the care of children needing supervision and care during the time parental care is not available. Such centers need not be publicly supported, though they should be scrupulously regulated, and public subsidies should be available for those who cannot be expected to pay their way. They should not be mandatory; there really are grandmothers and neighbors willing to help care for some children of working mothers. But where these are not available, the community children's care centers should be ready. We simply cannot afford to raise another generation of "key children," nor can we tolerate the numbers of children with no fixed abode found in many of our inner cities.

Second, radical changes must be made in our educational system. Children are now expected to be in school from about the age of six to about the age of eighteen, and many are encouraged to continue with higher education, even though interest and aptitude may be lacking. This implacably compulsory education results in some totally illiterate high-school graduates and in an alarming number of semiliterate college graduates. The illiteracy cannot be an isolated phenomenon; the values learned by the illiterate must be generally contrary to the interests of society as a whole as well as to the welfare of the individual himself. Surely the hostilities seen in so many schools—and the violence so often accompanying those hostilities

—must be due in part to the subjection of the individual to an educational process that does not seem related to his present or future circumstances.

Why continue this profitless compulsion? The answer is that we do not know what else to do with children between certain ages. We should repeal the child-labor laws and make work once again a responsible choice for a child and his parents. Once basic literacy and numeracy have been demonstrated—and these should not be a matter of choice—a boy or girl, from perhaps the age of twelve, thirteen, or fourteen, should have the right to choose work appropriate to his or her capacities. Obviously, the hours should not equal those worked by adults, and the pace should allow for the learning process on whatever job is undertaken. No child should be required to work, either by his parents or by the state, and at any time working children should be free to return to school. At the same time, schools should no longer be required to keep in attendance children who cannot or will not comply with the requirements of the classroom.

Putting this immense change into effect will require a fundamentally new conception of the nature of childhood and the expectations of the community regarding the role of the child as an unready human being. Employers will have to reorganize work forces; unions will have to adjust to entirely new working conditions and meet new challenges on behalf of junior members. The needed changes will require more imagination than I can offer at this point. But the benefits for all concerned will be better schools, happier children, and a community in which the habits of redundancy are at least being mastered.

Later in adolescence the third element of my plan should come into play: a policy of universal national service for youths. Some may choose the armed forces in which they will—unfortunately—be needed for many generations to come. Others may be involved in community services, in institutional services, and, perhaps, in such international services as the Peace Corps. For some, the obligation would be discharged after high-school graduation, or, for the working adolescent, after his eighteenth year. Others might be allowed to defer their service period until after college graduation, but no later. Properly organized, this program should demonstrate to everyone that no one is redundant in our society and that an enormous amount of work must be done if this country is to become a livable nation with a sense of national purpose. A second benefit will be the furtherance of solidarity among participants in the various national service programs. Loyalties to objectives and pride in the achievement of goals would be fostered.

This restructuring of our environment will be powerfully antidelinquent. If we have the national energy and will to tackle any program of this kind so vigorously that it actually succeeds, we should soon see a dramatic drop in the incidence of crime. It will not disappear. There will still be children who drift into delinquency and others whose mental, emotional, and social handicaps cannot be overcome by the changes in the patterns of childhood living I am proposing.

Instead of a juvenile court that prescribes treatment as well as determines guilt, such children need a juvenile division of the criminal court that determines responsibility for the criminal act as fairly and scrupulously as judges, lawyers, and juries possibly can. Once responsibility has been established, punishment should take place, but that punishment normally should be in the performance of services in the community and in the restriction of activities. Only for an offense so grave that a community sanction would be seen as insufficient and inappropriate would incarceration be used. The national service organizations may be able to absorb some of the delinquents and to provide guidance for those too immature or too refractory to be serving participants.

Suggesting changes as radical as these lays one open to charges of visionary impracticality. Many will contend that this country is not in such extreme straits that such revolutionary measures are needed. I fully expect my diagnosis to be tested by events ensuing from the continuation of our present attempts to meet the needs of youth. Those events will prove the social and institutional environment in which young people now grow up seriously obsolete. In an obsolete environment, inappropriate, malicious, and destructive behavior will continue and become even more aggravated. How much longer can society tolerate these antisocial pressures?

Notes

1. D. Moynihan, " 'Peace—' Some Thoughts on the 1960's and 1980's," the Forty-First Alfred E. Sterns Lecture, reprinted in *The Public Interest* 32 (1973):3-10.

2. Ibid., at p. 5.

3. Ibid., pp. 7-8.

4. *Newsweek*, March 23, 1981, pp. 46-54.

5. D. Moynihan, *supra* note 1, p. 8.

6. Ibid., p. 9.

7. For a particularly rich account of the "cool" style of life, see H. Feldman, M. Agar, and G. Beschner, *Angel Dust: An Ethnographic Study of PCP Users* (Lexington, Mass.: Lexington Books, D.C. Heath, 1979).

8. E. Banfield, *The Unheavenly City: The Nature and Future of Our Urban Crisis* (Boston: Little Brown, 1968), pp. 53-59.

Commentary

Stephen Chinlund

We gather today out of concern for our children and their crimes. Although there are fewer delinquent children today than ten or twenty years ago, they produce more disruption and violence than did their more numerous older brothers and sisters of yesterday. Many participants are here because they value those children but others only because they want crime to be reduced to make life more peaceful in society as a whole. We as a nation no longer value our young people; we do not like our children. Babies are adored, and postadolescent youth is admired, but the sprouting, awkward, infuriating, delightful, unpredictable centaur who is part child and part adult is seen almost entirely as a wretched problem.

Parents of children of that age are seen not as fortunate, but as deserving of sympathy. This cultural disease cannot be overemphasized. We need a new Norman Rockwell; we will never begin to solve in large numbers the problem of specific youngsters at risk until we have the wisdom and joy to be able to delight in our young people. Adolescence is as much a valley of delight as a tunnel of horrors, a fact our teenagers hope we learn soon. We undervalue human potential and overvalue the insulated peace that is the quiet of those fortified bunkers we call home. That is not peace, not the shalom of adventurous, respectful human interaction

We undervalue human service and overvalue technological efficiency. With each of these familiar distortions in values, the children suffer most. We will effectively reach out to those children who have reacted violently to our rejection, distrust, and hatred if we are aware of the negative cultural background out of which they see us coming.

These cold words must not turn into yet another way of avoiding the individuals who are now age six, ten, or twelve, cutting school, constantly fighting, clashing, and cutting their way through a life crowded by terrors, hoping as they cry in their beds at night that someone will find them. Look at them as they really are, recognize their misery, and show them the empathy that leads to a place where they will feel safe, where they will know they are needed and important, and where they will be able to love someone and be loved in return.

Many of the worst criminals were formerly "good" children. The choirboy syndrome of the well-behaved child becoming an ax murderer is not common, but it is a sufficiently frequent phenomenon to justify consideration in our planning. Much has been written and said about the problems of labeling youngsters as "predelinquent" or with any other such adjective that they quickly decode and use to devalue themselves and their future. We must use those methods we already know to keep heterogeneous groups of so-called good and bad together as long as possible for the benefit of all.

There is in all children, and in all adults, what I call a "heartiness quotient." This factor makes one either more or less able to cope with the pathogenic dimensions of home and school. Those with a low heartiness quotient get in trouble even though they have average parents and go to an average school. For them, average is not adequate. They are like albino children in the spring sunshine, for whom normal exposure to the sun is unbearable. On the other hand, those with high heartiness quotients can come through the most harrowing experiences—even child battering, incest, rape, and some of the psychic equivalents of the catalog of physical cruelty—clinging tenaciously to their souls in hope for a good life.

Just as there are criminals who once were choir boys, so too are there parents who look good superficially and yet inflict terrible harm on their children. Our strategies should seek those parents out and offer them that open road toward safety, a sense of being needed, and a place for love.

Logistical problems need not hamper our crusade. We must only be aware of the swamps and traps and try to avoid them. For example, a major spell cast over our land is the pervasiveness of a distorted ideal of competition. When everything is competitive, too little is cooperative. When too much is taken, too little is shared. The arena of cooperation and sharing can be enlarged through our strategies and the environment accordingly improved to the benefit of all.

So I turn to those strategies, built on the foundation of the human-potential movement: "Self-realization ain't all bad." Some foolish experiments and some ludicrous jargon have come out of that movement during the past twenty years, but that is true of every major human endeavor. The movement has matured, and among its enduring gifts to us is a profound respect for the capacity of human beings to continue to make choices for their own lives, even in prison or in other severely restricted situations. Another gift conferred by that movement is a new respect for the capacity of human beings to help each other, to be more fully alive, even without special training. All that is needed is a group structure and a leader trained to help the group meet productively so that the untrained people in the group can help each other.

Still another gift of the human potential movement is a reverence for pluralism. From colonial America to the present, our pluralism has usually been guarded and suspicious. We have tolerated other groups—although knowing that our group was right—because it was necessary to meet in order to carry on the business of civil government. Instead of hating others or other groups, the movement has luxuriated in those differences, finding in them inspiration for achieving greater clarity with regard to one's own personal choices.

One more gift among many others—one not uniquely that of the human-potential movement—is a clear vision of the complexity of human wholeness. No longer do we naively claim that some specific act will cure some complex area of human life. We know that physical illness and emotional life are profoundly intertwined. We know that having a good job is not a sufficient substitute for a satisfying family life. We know that academic and psychiatric professionals can no longer airily exlude ethical considerations from their work. Fractures of the whole person require holistic solutions.

I propose, as an environmental strategy, peer groups for people of all ages, for seasons of our lives during which we experience special stress or some other opportunity for growth. Such groups benefit all—even first-grade children—who are much more able to participate in such groups with creativity, purpose, and healing than anyone who has not experienced such a meeting would suppose.

With good leadership, those groups are especially helpful in primary and secondary schools in achieving clarity about one's own feelings, values, plans, and self-worth. The effectiveness of these groups is greatly enhanced if teachers and parents are engaged in similar activities, providing the maximum possibility for the creation of groups including parents, teachers, and students in cooperation. In this way, the at-risk child—whether identified externally or not, whether at risk to himself or not—will be served by the same process of becoming more human that serves the child who is not at risk.

Virginia Satir[1] and William Glasser,[2] among many others, have been particularly helpful in detailing some of the perspectives and techniques that make such groups work well. New life for such groups nourishes that most impoverished and most important of all groups, the American family. We lost our way, perhaps, in the 1920s when many new parents rebelled against the admittedly stifling rigidities of family life as it was then lived. Today, in many ways we are enlivening family structures or beginning to, resisting the erosion of time lost to television, minds lost to alcoholism, and hearts lost to drugs. Instead of these corrosives, some families are choosing a new simplicity of life, clearer communication, and an emphasis on love instead of consumer-crazed persona-building.

Beyond the creation of peer groups, we must enlarge the legitimate ways in which young people make themselves useful. For example, they can tutor younger children and provide other kinds of assistance in the lower-grade classroom. This device, used through the years by creative teachers, must now be regarded as a necessary part of any lively school. High-school students are also capable of providing volunteer services in old-people's homes, pediatric wards, and institutions for the severely retarded. It takes work, planning, and training to make such volunteer programs effective, but our souls are starved for failure to take on that hard work.

Existing programs in scouting, 4-H clubs, and our own Big Brother-Big Sister work have potential that far exceeds current achievement. In our search for new answers to the problem of children at risk, we must avoid making the same mistakes we accuse our children of making—namely, seeking simple solutions rather than those involving the necessary time, discipline, and hard work.

I endorse John Conrad's proposal to repeal the child-labor laws with major modifications. In fact, the law should not be repealed but changed to do certain things that are ultimately congruent with the thrust of his concern.

First, we must minimize exploitation by requiring that a child work more than one year in the same place. This would require employers to provide a continuing service for youth entering the job market. Second, and this differs from the Conrad proposals, we must require youngsters to attend school as a prerequisite to working: The work must be part-time. Prisons already house too many who proudly quit school at sixteen to put money on the family table. Too late, they realize that their siblings, who did not quit school, are now able to enter a job market closed to them. The dragon of competition—distorted competition—in which one's success is seen only in contrast with the failure of someone else remains. Admittedly, much of value in our land resulted from competition, but it was not a competition providing no hope to the bottom four-fifths of the class. Today, young people say, "If I am not at the top, it's all over for me."

Some people have a great need to sing their own song, do their own thing, and show their skills, without being limited to being basketball stars or physics prodigies. There could be, for example, a national Olympics with emphasis on the regional and subregional exposures, rather than competition, with a vast widening of the area of self-presentation. Beyond the usual athletic competitions, there could be chess and photography, weaving and music, and science fairs and theatrical productions. Unless we teach children early that they have something to give to the world, they will believe that they are redundant and will try to hurt those who put that label on them.

John Conrad's proposal of national service is one with which I thoroughly agree. It has been proposed many times over the years, and in many forms, but perhaps now it could be implemented. It would mean a whole new generation, educated in the need for human service and clear about the fact that a devotion to human beings need not bankrupt the nation. On the contrary, the nation may well go bankrupt if we fail to give such a program a higher priority than it now has.

Youth could work in forestry camps, prisons, and day-care centers. They could install solar units, create urban parks, and clean the subways. The work could be sufficiently diverse to include young men and women of all sizes and shapes, including the handicapped.

Preventing the venture from turning into a sloppy scene peopled by smokeheads trying to make an early career out of evasion of life is a great challenge, requiring brilliant leadership by inspiring people working together in a carefully developed organizational structure. But we have learned enough from the successes and failures of other smaller but similar ventures to go forward.

John Conrad's proposals for improved comprehensive day care for children of working parents and of A.D.C. parents and for restitution projects (especially for first-offender youths) are similarly congruent with his basic approach, and I support them. Like national service, both of these would take hard work and some money, although these proposals seem deceptively simple. They are already in operation, of course, in many places, but only where there is a deep commitment to high ideals for young people.

I acknowledge that small groups are no more a panacea for the ills of our society than is any other blueprint. The instinct of greedy competitiveness will not be easily obliterated. Perhaps it will only temporarily be held back from time to time from destroying all that we—society—hold dear. The struggle to help the youngsters caught between avarice and our love is worth our best imagination, our greatest energy, and our clearest planning.

Notes

1. V. Satir, *Peoplemaking* (Palo Alto, Calif.: Science and Behavior Books, 1972).

2. W. Glasser, *Schools Without Failure*, 1st ed. (New York: Harper & Row, 1969).

Commentary

Joseph Scott

Both Mr. Conrad and Mr. Chinlund indicate that the American system has failed to provide our youth the means for linking up with the economy and linking up with the other productive institutions in society. The youth have, indeed, been left out, made idle, and almost encouraged to be less than responsible.

We all agree that the economy has not expanded sufficiently and that the country has not had a policy of full employment and, indeed, does not even care to have such a policy. In many respects, therefore, all of this discussion is rather academic because when we finish, the kinds of proposals that follow from Mr. Conrad's discussion will not be forthcoming.

In an economy unable to provide enough jobs for teenagers, young adults, and even many older adults, the proposal to put mothers with children over two years of age into the labor force seems unrealistic. Who is going to hire them? At what jobs? And at what wages? The same can be said for the proposal to abolish child-labor laws; at a time when the country does not employ all able-bodied adults, how could putting children in the labor force help? This suggestion is like wishing pennies would fall from heaven. Maybe this is what we should discuss.

Mr. Conrad put great stress on the "the underclass," which by reference referred to the inner city, which is largely occupied by minorities: blacks and Hispanics, and now perhaps some Vietnamese. We often overlook the fact that this country is predominantly white, and any discussion of the *volume* of juvenile delinquency is mostly a discussion about white people. Nonetheless, the discussion almost always turns to blacks.

With regard to arrest rates, for example, whites predominate in five of the eight Part I National Crime Reports categories, which include the most serious of crimes, and blacks predominate in three. In Part II, minor offenses, whites predominate in twenty of the twenty-two categories.[1] Why, then, all this exclusive discussion about the underclass and blacks, and why all these statements that these people are "redundant," that they are "the most troublesome delinquents" and that they are "the most dangerous criminals"?

It has been suggested that children of the inner city be kept off the streets; that they have none of the skills that they need to survive in this world that has no use for them as they are; that the rowdies are mostly from the underclass; that the underclass produces the most alarming young delinquents; that this group (young delinquents) is a class of impoverished, idle youth who engage in actions that are destructive and potentially lethal; that inner-city schools are characterized by disorder, intimidation, attacks on teachers, and terrorism; and that the values learned by these illiterates must be contrary to the interests of society as a whole. Well, I have difficulty with all of that. The ethnic composition of the Michigan community in which I grew up was predominantly Polish and East European. Nonetheless, crime, attacks on teachers, and vandalism were everyday occurrences.

I now live in a middle-class area made up of $90,000 houses, surrounded by middle-class people whose children cut the screens out of your houses, drive across your lawns with their cars, and steal things out of your garage and out of your yard. Fifty percent of the children in the local high school come from professional families. The category that the students themselves call "the rowdies" in the local high school are the upper-middle-class kids.

To be sure, the members of the so-called underclass have special problems, but their problems and behaviors might be exaggerated. We are naive to focus primarily or particularly on this group and lose sight of the more general causes, the more general kinds of things that Mr. Chinlund mentioned: that is, what is happening to youth in general, how we are treating youth in general, and how youth are generally manifesting their youth culturally at this point in our history.

When we talk about the youth culture as being selfish, callous, and sinister, we forget that it was the same youth group, born after World War II and coming of age in the sixties, who got us out of the Vietnam War morass. It was this group that helped us realize the personal-growth movement in this country. These were the youth with idealism and with notions of self-expression and self-actualization that freed us all. The research clearly shows that youth leading the free-speech movement and other freedom movements were not the poorer academic students, but the better academic students. This same group gave us the yippie and hippie movements: As a result, many of us now wear beards, and some of us have adopted other values of that generation. Many of us see some truth in their criticism of the system and of our devotion to the Protestant ethic to the exclusion of all other life philosophies. The rise of the youth culture, therefore, was not all bad; not only did the youth not lead us astray, they have been good and important for society, as a whole.

At the same time, while there developed in this country a general youth culture and, most assuredly, a lower-class youth culture, only a few of us were writing about the development of the new middle-class youth culture.[2] In the late fifties and early sixties, middle-class kids for the first time in our history had time on their hands and were able to establish a street-corner society, much like the lower-class kids had already established. While we think of middle-class subculture primarily in terms of sex, drugs, drinking, and automobiles (in contrast to the underclass's theft, burglary, and robbery), the middle-class youth culture is very alive and thriving and should not be overlooked in a complete analysis. Delinquent subculture does not reside primarily in the working class or lower class of this society. We must deal with the whole youth culture—both in middle-class and lower-class areas—and see how it recruits, trains, or promotes certain kinds of antisocial behavior in society.

The socioeconomic issue in our society is crucial. Nearly half of all the poor families in the United States are headed by one person in the labor force, but they are still poor. Eighty-two percent of male heads of poor families are in the labor force. For families with female heads the participation is less. For such male heads between the ages of twenty-five and sixty-four, over 90 percent participate in the labor force, and 60 percent hold full-time jobs.[3] Even, therefore, while we talk about putting mothers and children to work, we have heads of families working full time for poverty-level wages.

Very often, these discussions turn to blaming the victims. Decisions about the utilization of labor in this country are not made by the poor themselves, but by management and government. Yet management and government have not seen fit to devise a way by which even adults willing to work can make a living wage.

The demand for labor, and more specifically the demand for unskilled labor, is not a decision that the poor make. As a result, the poor in this country are forced to shuttle among jobs, unemployment, and welfare. We then condemn them for being on welfare, for being redundant, and for producing an inordinate number of troublesome youth.

It was stated that the children in the so-called less-comfortable classes have no economic value, yet statistics indicate that 60 percent of all families have a full-time working head; this includes 62 percent of white families and 47 percent of black families. Seventy-four percent of white families who have two earners and 66 percent of black families who have two earners have a full-time working head. Eighty-four percent of white families who have four persons working and 76 percent of black families who have four earners, have a full-time working head. These same statistics indicate that the black wife's contribution constitutes a greater portion of the family's income than does the income of the white wife.[4]

These data also suggest that the only way for black families to get beyond poverty is through having more than one earner, that is, a child or a wife or both in the labor force, in addition to the male head. The economic value of such a child, therefore, is considerable.

Most of the people in the less-comfortable classes try their best, given our society, to be good citizens and to bring their children up with sound moral values. It therefore bothers me to see whole categories of people condemned, blasphemed, labeled, and charged with all of the ills of our society.

I support a policy of full employment, a policy of paying every able-bodied worker a living wage. Poverty is not a result of full employment but the result of no wages and often low wages. A national full-employment policy would solve many of the delinquency problems we are discussing.

I agree with Mr. Conrad that we should be looking at whole categories of children who are at risk. We can identify criminogenic processes in society, that is to say, processes that promote antisocial behavior. For example, much of the youth-culture contents, of both the lower class and the middle class, can promote antisocial behavior harmful to society.

Factors such as school failure, family instability, extreme economic deprivation, and child abuse present criminogenic situations calling for action. We need not wait for children to manifest negative behavior to identify those who are at risk. We must categorically treat all of the children in these criminogenic situations. Perhaps the positive peer culture approach that has been introduced into a few correctional institutions—an approach calling for a new value system, a new behavior mode, and, of course, a new reward system for acting decently—offers us hope. If we can reverse the criminogenic processes in American society that contribute to the rising incidence of antisocial behavior and juvenile delinquency, we can decrease juvenile delinquency. Let us start with social structures first.

Notes

1. *Uniform Crime Reports* (Washington, D.C.: U.S. Government Printing Office, 1977), pp. 184-186.

2. J.W. Scott and E. Vaz, "A Perspective on Middle-Class Delinquency," *The Canadian Journal of Economics and Political Science* 29, no. 3 (1963):324-335.

3. B.R. Schiller, *The Economics of Poverty and Discrimination*, 2d ed. (Englewood Cliffs, N.J.: Prentice-Hall, 1976), pp. 33-34.

4. *Statistical Abstract of the United States*, 99th ed. (Washington, D.C.: U.S. Government Printing Office, 1978), pp. 457, 459.

Roundtable

Conrad: Altruism alone will not do the job. We need an economic structure that will support the altruism and make possible the full participation of everyone in the economy rather than the modified participation and non-participation on the part of so many.

I am pleased that Dr. Scott agrees with me at least on the basic principle—namely, that we must examine the processes that create misery in American society, including not only crime, which we hear most about, but much apathy and, as I put it, lives not worth living and perceived as such. I must agree with Scott that the present political and economic climate make unlikely in the near future the realization of many of my proposals. The solutions currently offered in Washington and elsewhere, however, are very likely not going to work as well as advertised. Something else will be needed. Unfortunately, the present economy makes likely an increasing number of people dependent on welfare or on their wits for survival, a situation presenting obvious risks to society.

I did not say and I want to emphasize that I do not think that young women should work as soon as their dependents are two years old, unless they wish to. I am appalled by the Washington suggestion that strenuous measures should be taken to induce women to leave the A.F.D.C. roll as soon as their children are two years old. Indeed, women must have some responsibility for their children long after the age of two, and for many women it is more important to stay home and take care of their childen than to be forced into the labor market.

I do not use the term *redundant* as a value judgment, nor do I think a person is redundant through his own choice. But there are people in our society who are redundant as far as the economy is concerned and whose parents and grandparents before them were similarly redundant. That there are too many of these people is not the fault of those people but of the economy.

I still contend that to many families, and to most lower-income families, the economic value of children is not great. Admittedly, many kids in poorer families bring home some money, but it is not economically very significant.

I am not condemning. I am not labeling. I only point out that members of the underclass are limited to a tragically narrow band of choices and are outside the security system of insurance schemes, social security, and the like, which protect people from higher classes.

The poor do not cause the most serious ills in our society, for example, the Vietnam War, Watergate, or major economic crimes. But the poor—both black and white—are vastly overrepresented in the incidence of violent crime. That the majority of the people in the underclass are not criminals deserves emphasis but does not excuse America from making a strenuous effort to bring the underclass into the economy as producing members. If everybody were producing in a productive economy, the crime problem bringing us together today would not warrant our meeting ten years from now.

Lazar: Professor Conrad gives us a comfortable mythology. Certainly, more people from low-economic neighborhoods than from middle-class neighborhoods are convicted of violent crime. This reflects the inequality of opportunity in our society. It was not an underclass person who shot the president, it is not underclass people generally who traffic dope, it is not underclass people who represent the majority of crime in the United States.

For the last thirty years, work (the production of goods) has increasingly become obsolete as a human activity. The development of technology, spurred on by tax provisions to encourage investment, has resulted in more automated work, thus eliminating more jobs. We are told, "Look at all the jobs in *The New York Times* and the *Washington Post*." Certainly, anyone who can read computer language can get one of those jobs. But our school system has been obsolete for a long time. A new kind of institution for the group care of children and adolescents during daytime hours will develop, because we can teach basic skills at home with a microprocessor better than we now do in the public-school system. An institution that loses 40 percent of its clients and does not charge for its services has something radically wrong with it.

We continue to lose jobs but have no real intention either to substitute a system of guaranteed work (as do most European countries, in which government is the employer of last resort) or to tolerate a system in which not everyone has to work. We cling to the work ethic but refuse to do what other civilized countries do to ensure that the work ethic pays off.

One especially disturbing myth is that many families have been on welfare for generations. The average stay on welfare in the United States is two years, up from ten years ago when it was only eighteen months. The turnover is enormous because most people do not want to be on welfare. Indeed, the major users of food stamps in the United States under current rules are military families and men.

It is interesting to point out that a single parent with two children receives about $300 more a month by working than by not working and drawing benefits. Some current proposals from Washington would reduce that differential.

Every Western nation but ours has a guaranteed-income plan or family-allowance plan. Since everyone gets it, there is no bureaucracy dealing with eligibility. The income-tax system recaptures the money from those who do not need it.

Gilman: Perhaps we should guarantee work and income, but even in countries doing such things (for example, Sweden, West Germany, and Japan) there is a rising rate of crime, alcoholism, suicide, and dissatisfied youth. In short, such economic programs are desirable but will not cure the delinquency problem we are addressing.

Conrad: I must disagree. The incidence of crime in Japan has consistently gone down for the last twenty years and is still low compared to that in the United States. Despite a disturbing incidence of alcoholism and suicide, Sweden has a very low incidence of violent crime.

Scott: We must remember that we are talking about different kinds of crimes. White-collar crimes, after all, are committed by people with money. But providing jobs and raising the socioeconomic level might shift the kind of crime. In bad economic times, robbery, burglary, and other theft-type and related crimes increase. On the other hand, in better economic times, drug crimes might increase because people have more money to buy cocaine and the like.

Gilman: Politically, our concern tends to be limited to lower-class crimes. As a society, we tolerate white-collar crimes.

Stroud: Our discussion seems to have shifted from intervening with the child to intervening in a whole economy. Those are two quite different problems. If it is so difficult to intervene with a juvenile delinquent using orthodox methods and our current bureaucratic agencies, how do we expect to secure child-care centers and full employment?

Conrad: For many years, I have been involved in and have observed various kinds of social programs addressing juvenile delinquency. Most of them have been very unproductive. We must develop a full-employment economy in order to reduce the kinds of crime that induce fear and anxiety.

Lazar: Behavior takes place not in isolation, but in a physical, social ecology. The behavior of disturbed and antisocial children is often a reasonable response to an unreasonable life situation. No amount of intervention with individuals will work if we send them back into a destructive life situation. We must send them back to something better.

Chinlund: That is often, but not always, true. There are as many criminally minded people—children and adults—in the upper and middle classes as there are in the lower classes. They act in different ways, but they all act on those impulses, impulses related in very hazy ways to full employment. I believe in full employment; but there are people raised by parents who have not been fully employed who credit their own strength, values, and determination to watching their parents deal with poverty. Until we deal with our crisis of values, we will increasingly have trouble with our kids, who sense that we do not know what we want.

Scott: Full employment is critical to the reinforcement of the values we want our children to have. Sociologically, work is a form of discipline, of social control, and of value reinforcement. We have a crisis of values because our values are not anchored to anything. To a kid who is not working or even encouraged to work and who does not have to deprive himself in order to save money, the Protestant ethic is just so much idealism. In a full-employment economy, in which the work ethic and ancillary values such as savings and the like are strong and properly reinforced, affluent kids will commit fewer crimes (such as shoplifing, drug use, and joy riding) because of idleness and will commit fewer thefts for expressive, as opposed to utilitarian, purposes.

Lindgren: John Conrad's suggestion of universal service, one very much worth exploring, does have problems. Current values, including an antidraft sentiment, run opposite. Such a program, however, would greatly help in staffing small correctional programs and the like and in keeping them on the ideal plane that bureaucratic organizations tend to drift away from.

I would emphasize the real difference between crimes of violence, which cause the fear, and others. That difference is a reality, not a myth, and it is the fear-inducing crime that moves the state to intervene and undermines the daily existence of people living in such fear. The likelihood, for example, of a young black male in the ghetto dying a violent death is alarmingly high. This situation cannot be dismissed as differential enforcement or as a myth.

Hopson: Earlier, we mentioned the need for pluralism, for democracy, and for noncoercive intervention. Speaking now on the large level, are we willing to talk about putting children in ''jail'' (that is, drafting them into a universal service program)? We talk about the work ethic and individual values but not about whether one *wants* to work or not. I am not sure we are consistent.

Part IV
Discovery of a Child at Risk

Discovery of Children at Risk for Juvenile Delinquency

Brandt F. Steele

Although the details of what is called juvenile delinquency vary from time to time and in various jurisdictions and in different countries, all of us share some general ideas of the antisocial behaviors of youths. We are quite used to reading distressed commentaries such as the following:

> In all civilized lands criminal statistics show two sad and significant facts: first that there is a marked increase of crime at the age of 12-14 years, not in crimes of one, but all kinds, and that this increase continues for a number of years. While the percentages of certain grave crimes increase to mature manhood, adolescence is preeminently the criminal age when most first commitments occur and most vicious careers are begun. The second fact is that the proportion of juvenile delinquents seems to be everywhere increasing and crime is more and more precocious.

This note, which sounds so contemporary, was written by G. Stanley Hall in 1904,[1] long before television, Vietnam, or the recent drug scene.

Hall also noted that Germany in 1892 had over 46,000 juvenile convicts and an increase of 50 percent by 1895. Forty-one percent of all German criminals were under twenty-one years of age. A hundred years ago in France, as many were sentenced for crimes committed between the ages of sixteen and twenty as between twenty and forty. In New York in 1823, among a population of 132,000, 1,650 persons, of which one-third were under twenty-one, were charged for crimes. This is an old phenomenon.[2] Clay tablets from 2,500 years ago in ancient Sumer record the whipping or caning of disobedient schoolboys.[3] And 6,000 years ago in ancient Egypt, an unhappy priest carved on a stone pillar: "Our earth is degenerate. . . . children no longer obey their parents."[4]

Probably never in history have children obeyed their parents completely or been free of misbehavior, and there have always been attempts to understand and deal with the problem in two different frameworks: (1) that of the "crime," and (2) that of the "criminal." The records of juvenile delinquents suggest that much more attention is given to the crime than to the alleged criminal. There is copious documentation of misbehaviors at home and at school, of stealing, of assaults, of running away, and the like, but there is little or nothing about the youngster and his total life except the simplest demographic and identification data. The significance of the episode and the disposition of the case depend on the seriousness of the assault and personal injury, the value of property involved, and the repetitiveness of the acts.

Complications in this simplistic evaluation appear when the age of the child is considered. What might be charged as assault and battery in adolescence or adulthood would be considered not unexpected fighting on occasions in childhood, fighting that we expect will be outgrown or restrained by educational persuasions, scolding, or mild punishment. A certain amount of lying and of stealing cookies, candy, toys, and loose change are essentially normal events in the early childhood development. Such events occur whether the child is growing up in a poverty-stricken ghetto or in a high-class, wealthy suburb. The difficult question is why such a prevalent, almost universal kind of early childhood behavior changes for the better in most of us but persists in a small proportion of children, becoming the antisocial activity that we call delinquency and criminality.

Many so-called causes have been blamed for this phenomenon, ranging from the obviously harmful influences of poverty, poor education, and other socioeconomic factors to the individual family problems of broken homes, absent fathers, alcoholism, unemployment, drug addiction, excessive mobility, and exposure to bad companions and gangs. Causes more specifically bearing on the individual include the concept of an innately "bad character" due to poor heredity, to some kind of subtle brain damage or to a weak character or deliberately evil, rebellious disposition. Rather than discuss the enormous literature on these subjects with which many readers are quite familiar, I will discuss the development of delinquency from my particular bias as a psychoanalytic student of infant and child development. A developmental approach gives us one means of early detection of high-risk individuals and thereby opens the way toward intervention and prevention.

For the past twenty years, I have worked with families involved in the unhappy situations of child abuse and neglect. Although such maltreatment of children is in itself a form of antisocial behavior, it is not ordinarily considered among the usual categories of delinquency or criminality unless a child is very seriously injured or killed. Instead of producing the healthiest, most capable offspring to become the adults of the next generation, parents indulging in these very maladaptive forms of behavior produce children in some degree impaired in their emotional, cognitive, and social development. Many such maltreated children, not too severely damaged by their parents and helped by other more beneficent environmental factors, become adequately healthy adults who integrate sufficiently well into society, but many others are permanently damaged. Of great interest is the finding that maltreating parents almost always were themselves victims of significant neglect, with or without physical abuse, in their own earliest years. We thus have an example of the influence of early life experience on later behavior and can use the evaluation of early life as an indication of high-risk for somewhat difficult parenting behaviors.

What does this phenomenon of child abuse have to do with juvenile delinquency? Some maltreating parents have either a present or past history of delinquency, but many others show no signs of any antisocial activity besides their maltreatment patterns. Hence, there is no one-to-one relationship between being delinquent and being a child abuser. There are, however, other ways of finding a possible relationship between the two behaviors. Twelve or more years ago, James Weston, working with the problems of child abuse in Philadelphia, told me that in-depth interviews with one hundred consecutive juvenile offenders revealed that 80 percent of them had a history of being neglected or abused as young children, and 40 percent could recall being knocked unconscious by one or the other parent. I was very impressed, although not surprised, by this finding, since I was already familiar with reports indicating that murderers usually gave histories of exposure to violence, neglect, and abuse in early life and of delinquency in those earlier years.

I wondered, however, if Weston's data were significantly skewed by being obtained in a core city area with profound socioeconomic problems and if, therefore, things would be different in, say, Colorado. I encouraged my co-worker, Joann Hopkins, to undertake a study of youngsters at a detention center to which all juveniles picked up in the county by police were brought for evaluation, court hearing, and disposition. This detention center, generously made available for our study, is in a county adjacent to metropolitan Denver. The county has a mixture of dense, urban sections with both middle- and lower-class components, suburban areas with both middle- and upper-class residents, small towns, and rural farm and ranch areas. There is some medium and light industry. The population is predominantly Anglo with a significant number (14 percent) of Spanish-named families and a few blacks (1/2 percent). Adjacent to the county is a large military establishment. About one-fifth of the population is below the $14,000 income level, with the rest well above that level.

Hopkins interviewed a randomly chosen sample of two hundred youngsters soon after they were picked up for the first time (that is, before any labeling or other "contamination" by the system) by law-enforcement officers for offenses ranging from runaway (70 percent) through truancy, stealing, assault, robbery, breaking and entering, and homicide (1 case). For one hundred of these cases, corroborative information was obtained from parents, other relatives, social agencies, schools, and law-enforcement records. For the remaining 100 cases, information was obtained only from the youngster. Ages, types of offense, home location, and socioeconomic status were not significantly or consistently different in the two groups. The results are of special interest and value because the population studied is quite different from that involved in the more commonly reported evaluations of urban, core-city, ghetto, and minority groups.

The determination of abuse in early childhood required as a minimum the existence of significant bruising on the buttocks or elsewhere before the child had started school. Other more serious physical traumas and neglect were also reported. Of the one hundred cases for which no corroborative evidence was available, seventy-six reported abuse before school age. Abuse before school age was reported in 85 percent of those cases for which corroborative information was obtained in addition to the youth's own statement. Even more remarkably, 92 percent had been bruised, lacerated, or fractured by a parent within the year and a half previous to the pickup. In addition to the common pattern of children running away from a physically abusive situation, about one-half of the runaway girls were escaping from incest.

Not all of this information was gathered in a single interview. Some of the children, picked up as repeaters, gave more details of previous abuse and incest on subsequent interviews when more trust in the interviewer had developed. Some of the children were included in the abused group even though they themselves denied being abused, considering their severe maltreatment as "deserved" because they were "bad." These two studies are essentially valid although they are open to the criticism of being only retrospective and therefore subject to errors of memory and recall.

Evidence linking early-life neglect and abuse to later delinquency has been derived in a very different kind of study carried out by Jackie Howell of the Juvenile Division of the Los Angeles Police Department. The names of a cohort of seventeen-year-old juvenile offenders were checked through state and local records for previous reports of contacts with official agencies. A significant percentage of these delinquent youths had had their first contact recorded in their early years as being a dependent child because of abuse or neglect. Howell, too, thinks that probably 80 to 90 percent of juvenile delinquents were victims of maltreatment in early life.

Unfortunately, none of these three studies has been published. A fourth study of the same problem, however, published by the Select Committee on Child Abuse of the State Assembly of New York, indicates an empirical relationship between child abuse and later socially deviant behavior.[5] Similar to the Los Angeles study, and based on a review of the official records of child protection agencies and of the courts of eight counties in New York state, it demonstrated that "a considerable percentage of children" in the 1950s and 1970s samples "were abused or neglected and reported as delinquent or ungovernable when they were older." Among the more important findings were the following:

1. "As many as 50% of the families reported for child abuse and neglect had at least one child who was later taken to court as delinquent or ungovernable."[6] "In the county with the most complete set of records, Monroe County, 64% of the families were in this situation."[7]
2. "In Monroe County, the rate of juvenile delinquency and ungovernability among the children reported as abused and neglected was 5 times greater than among the general population."[8]
3. "In three counties, 35% of the boys and 44% of the girls reported to a court as delinquent or ungovernable in the early 1970s had been reported previously as abused or neglected."[9]

Since abuse and neglect are incompletely reported at the present time and were reported far less frequently in the years prior to 1970, the official reports of abuse were doubtless much lower than the actual incidence.

These studies uniformly indicate some kind of connection between child maltreatment and later socially deviant behavior, but it is obviously not a one-to-one relationship and certainly it cannot be said simplistically that child abuse causes delinquency. Many other socioeconomic factors and interpersonal relationships within and without the family also will affect the child's life, enhancing or diminishing the development of delinquency and influencing the time of onset and the type of the antisocial behavior. Yet if this assumption of a connection is valid, it should be possible to demonstrate some threads of continuity between the early abuse and the later delinquency. Our own work with maltreated infants has revealed the appearance of certain psychological states and patterns that become embedded in the child's personality development and make him at high risk for or prone to the later appearance of delinquency.

The child-abuse syndrome can be understood as a disorder of the closely related phenomena of attachment and empathy. Because of deprivation in her own early life, a mother is unable to attach fully to her new baby. (While my discussion at this point will focus on the mother, a similar phenomenon can occur in connection with fathers.) In the absence of good attachment, the mother cannot provide adequate empathic care. She thus brings up an emotionally deprived baby who will grow up to be a parent who attaches poorly and cannot provide empathic care. And so the cycle tends to repeat itself from generation to generation.

But lack of empathy is not only evidenced in patterns of child care. It appears to a greater or lesser extent in all of the person's human relationships. If it is accompanied by great neediness, it leads to thoughtless, uncaring exploitation and misuse of other persons, prime characteristics of delinquents. We describe these people as selfish, taking what they want without regard for the rights of others. Thus deprivation in the earliest months plus the identification with unempathic caretakers contributes to later delinquent behavior. This cold, uncaring quality has been succinctly described by the eighteenth century Irish dramatist, Isaac Bickerstaffe, who wrote, "I care for nobody, not I, if no one cares for me."[10]

One manifestation of the lack of empathy is the mother's failure to respond appropriately to her infant's signals of hunger, cold, need for sleep, or wish for company. Her caretaking is inconsistent, irregular, and unpredictable. For instance, when the infant is hungry, on one occasion she will feed him; the next time, he is punished for crying. Other interactions in caretaking are equally insensitive and disruptive. Under these circumstances, the infant or child cannot develop basic trust or any confidence that adults, especially authorities, will be good to him, not an unusual finding in delinquents. More subtly, the inconsistent caretaking seen in neglect and abuse cases deprives the infant of the chance to develop a sense of reliable relationships between inner feelings and a response from the environment. He cannot trust "himself" and has trouble developing a solid identity. Similarly, his self-esteem is lowered, and it is damaged even more by later parental criticism and disregard. Abused children are punished because they try to follow their own desires or needs and soon learn to disregard their own feelings and adapt to the demands of their caretakers. Their own inner controls are abandoned in favor of paying attention to cues and clues from the environment.

The unreliability of the signal response system in the caretaker-infant interaction interferes with the infant's cognitive development. He cannot learn through reliable repetition of caretaker responses to his signals. He does not learn that "A" is associated with "B," and thus primary development of the symbolic functions is interfered with. Learning in general and language development in particular can be seriously disrupted, as is seen in many neglected and abused children. They are the ones who flunk kindergarten and first grade and who make up a significant proportion of the children in special-education classes.

The coexistence of school difficulties and delinquency has been recognized for years, although, as exemplified by the 1976 U.S. Department of Justice report, "The Link Between Learning Disabilities and Juvenile Delinquency," it has been poorly understood. This report depicts the lack of agreement on definitions and types of learning disability and could not establish a reliable understanding of the link between the two phenomena. I personally believe that studies of child abuse and delinquent development through the channel of learning disability can help segregate at least one clear pattern of this relationship.

Fifteen years ago, Conger and others described the personality characteristics, noted in boys as early as kindergarten to third grade, associated with later delinquency.[11] These personality characteristics are familiar ones in our maltreated children, although the authors did not make that connection. Often, scholastic difficulties are accompanied by various aggressive behaviors in the predelinquent years, and such aggressive activity, too, often has its roots in the early experience of a chaotic, abusive environment. A clear picture of this is given by a thirty-three-year-old, aggressive criminal who had been delinquent since age ten or twelve and had spent a third of his life in prison.

> [V]iolence is in a way like bad language—something that a person like me has been brought up with. Something I got used to very early on as a part of the daily scene of childhood, you might say. I don't at all recoil from the idea. I don't have a sort of inborn dislike of the thing like you do. As long as I can remember, I have seen violence in use all around me—my mother hitting the children; my brothers and sisters all whacking one another, or other children; the man downstairs bashing his wife, etc. You get used to it. It doesn't mean anything in these circumstances.[12]

While early neglect and abuse is only one of the many factors involved in development of later delinquency, it is possibly the earliest and most important matrix, providing a fertile ground in which all the other deleterious influences may take root and flourish: the low self-esteem that makes a youngster ready to do anything to gain respect or status; a lack of emphatic consideration for others; a lack of identity and inner controls; a built-in readiness to allow orders from others to guide actions; learning difficulties; and a readiness to discharge aggression. All of these combine to pave the way to delinquency and to joining up with bad companions, especially when the child enters the period of normal rebellion against authority coupled with the desire to escape abuse and neglect in an environment seen as uncaring.

I have tried to demonstrate the prevalence and importance of child maltreatment as an early precursor of delinquency in order to support my belief that detection of children at risk for delinquency can be roughly equated with our efforts to detect children at high risk for abuse and neglect. Although our ability is far from perfect, a growing body of experience helps us predict the potential for poor parenting or maltreatment in a family, or to discover, as we say in euphemistic but more acceptable terms, "families in need of special services." Prediction of high-risk families enables us to focus our preventive interventions where they are most productive. Data indicate that intervention significantly reduces the expected amount of serious neglect and abuse in high-risk families compared to that in similar high-risk families receiving routine care without special intervention. Observations of parents and parent-infant interactions in the prenatal period, and especially during labor, delivery, and early postpartum provide the most accurate predictive information. This is a noninvasive, undisturbing technique easily carried out by regular personnel who have had extra training in what to look for.[13]

The simple interventions found to be effective involve follow-up care provided by one rather than several different physicians and regular home visits by specially oriented public-health nurses and/or trained lay health visitors.[14] This is not unlike the situation in those countries that, having compulsory health systems, provide such care universally, and in which child-abuse incidence is lower than in the United States.[15] Later, nonpunitive intervention in families at the appearance of the first signs of neglect or abuse can also prevent further trouble but is more difficult. If intervention is delayed until children are already in the delinquent pattern, it is extremely difficult and often ineffectual.

An added advantage to using the association of maltreatment and delinquency as a tool of early detection of high-risk children is that the means of easily obtaining the needed information already exist in medical and hospital personnel and in the social agencies. Some special training in observation may be needed, but there is no necessity for creating new organizations or specialties.

It would be naive to suppose that the problems of juvenile delinquency could be solved by the use of early detection of high-risk children in the child-abuse situation. But if we really want to reduce the human anguish and economic costs of delinquency and crime, we would likely do well to begin monitoring the care of children in their earliest months of life.

Notes

1. T.S. Hall, *Adolescence: Its Psychology and Its Relation to Physiology, Anthropology, Sex, Crime, Religion and Education*, vols. 1 and 2, (New York and London: D. Appleton, 1917), (1st ed. 1904), pp. 325-329.

2. Ibid.

3. N. Kramer, *From the Tablets of Sumer* (Indian Hills, Co.: The Falcon's Wing Press, 1956), pp. 8, 11.

4. Quoted by Adelaide Johnson, "Juvenile Delinquency," *American Handbook of Psychiatry*, ed., S. Arieti (New York: Basic Books, 1959), p. 840.

5. See the Assembly, State of New York, Select Committee on Child Abuse, *Summary Report on the Relationship Between Child Abuse and Neglect and Later Socially Deviant Behavior* (New York: Select Committee on Child Abuse, 1978).

6. Ibid., p. 11.

7. Ibid.

8. Ibid., p. 12.

9. Ibid., p. 15.

10. I. Bickerstaffe, *Love in a Village*, Act 1, sc. 5.

11. J. Conger and W. Miller, *Personality, Social Class and Delinquency* (New York: Wiley, 1966), pp. 533-559.

12. T. Parker and R. Allerton, *The Courage of His Convictions* (New York: W.W. Norton, 1962), p. 93.

13. J. Gray, C. Cutler, J. Dean, and C.H. Kempe, "Perinatal Assessment of Mother-Baby Interactions," in *Child Abuse and Neglect: The Family and the Community*, eds. R. Helfer and C.H. Kempe (Cambridge, Mass.: Ballinger, 1976).

14. See J. Gray, C. Cutler, J. Dean, and C.H. Kempe, "Prediction and Prevention of Child Abuse and Neglect," *Child Abuse and Neglect* 1 (1977):45; J. Gray and B. Kaplan, "The Lay Health Visitor Program," in *The Battered Child*, 3rd ed., eds. C.H. Kempe and R. Helfer (Chicago: University of Chicago Press, 1980). Also, the author has worked with families of abused children and has witnessed complete changes in parenting patterns in formerly abusive parents.

15. Some sixteen years ago, Sweden made corporal punishment in the schools illegal and, six years ago, extended the ban to include corporal punishment in the home. This, as well as economic factors, may have a bearing on Sweden's lower incidence of crime.

Commentary

Irving Lazar

I am uncomfortable with the term *juvenile delinquent*. As I think about behaviors that concern us, what we mean by "delinquent" is always defined in terms of the range of socially accepted behaviors of young people in a given community at a given time. The more densely populated and complicated a community, the narrower the range of acceptable behaviors, and therefore, by definition, the higher the rate of delinquency and the incidence of delinquent behavior. What were pranks in my childhood are crimes today. Because of this absolutely locational and temporal definition of delinquency, we can easily be led away from looking at causes to focusing only on transient symptoms. If we just wanted to prevent delinquency, for example, we could do worse than simply moving everyone into communities no larger than 25,000: There is a convincing correlation of delinquency with population density.

The real problem is matching the demands of the society to the adaptive capacities of children. How can we better insure successful and increasing socialization for tomorrow's world? We are born in very strange kinds of situations for mammals—particularly for carnivores. We are the most helpless of creatures at first. Each creature has a kind of trade-off between its ability to survive at birth and its adapatability to later change in its environment: The better equipped it is to survive at birth, the more dependent it is on an unchanging environment.

The human path of development has been to maximize our adaptability to change, but that makes us more helpless in the beginning and more dependent on protection and teaching from older members of our species.

The trade for adaptability that we make is responsibility. What we call *delinquent* is a transient local derivative of what we call *adjustment* in a transient local situation. I believe that the limits of acceptable behavior are finite, but very broad. The basic responsibility for defining limits lies with adults, and first of all with the parent or primary caretaker. We know that the earlier we can start the socialization process, the easier and more successful it is. A lot of data, about some of which more will be said later, support that generalization.

What does the developmental literature tell us about promoting appropriate socialization? The first and most important single consideration is the presence of an adult who cares: an adult who is irrationally attached to the child, who loves the child, and who promotes his increasing independence. Second, the research literature and clinical experience tell us that such care must continue throughout the child's early years. One cannot keep switching partners. Third, the rules of life in the society and in the family must be presented at a rate at which the child can learn. There have to be rewards for compliance and consequences that make sense at a level the child can understand.

There needs to be respect for a child's accomplishments. He needs to feel himself a worthwhile person with a reasonable hope for success, both in the short-term and in the long-term. Compliance with social demands must continue to pay off. We need to provide children with clear models of desired behavior.

Who, then, is at risk? I would propose that the at-risk population includes those children who do not have these basic conditions at the beginning and during the course of their lives.

Starting at the beginning, let us assume that a child, wanted and loved, is born to a pair of parents who have not the foggiest idea of how children grow, how they learn, or what to do with them—not an unusual situation. Life and child rearing have become too complex for such simple instincts as we are born with to carry us through the parental process. All of us have met parents who were devastating to their children despite their well-meaning intentions. Consequently, the first step in a preventive program ought to be the teaching of parenting in the elementary schools, at the ages before sexuality clouds the child's understanding of parenthood. In view of the subjects cluttering up the elementary-school curriculum, we could find room to do a decent job of introducing youngsters to the responsibilities and meanings of parenthood and to the development of parenting skills. Children will not resist such learning.

Indeed, one of the most interesting day-care operations I have ever visited is attached to a public school. Elementary-school children work with younger children in a mutual-help arrangement that is built into the day-care operation. For example, third-graders who are having trouble with reading are sent to read to the three-year olds. From the three-year-olds' point of view, the third-graders read marvelously. Therefore, the three-year olds give real support to the third-graders. To read to three-year-olds, however, does not cause the third-grader to "lose face" with his peers while he increases his reading skills.

A child's character is not inborn; it is based on learning. We learn from our parents, and as parents we practice what we learned from our parents because, usually, it is the only way we know. It is this modelling that produces, for example, the generational transmission of abuse, of neglect, and of lack of affection and contact, as Dr. Steele stated and beautifully illustrated. The home is the first place in which we can do parenting education, and the first place in which we can do prevention.

Because a caring adult is the child's first crucial requirement, we should not require that anyone become a parent. Childbirth should be a positive choice and not a punitive consequence of lust. The child who from the start is not wanted is at risk for wreckage. If the society at large or certain religions insist that all conceptions be carried to term, they must also take responsibility for competent and caring socialization by an adult who wants to take on that very difficult job.

We can discuss separately several options for encouraging and ensuring positive choices, but the first line of prevention is obviously the ready availability of both contraception and abortions and adequate machinery for the prompt adoption of children who are not wanted.

Last year, we almost succeeded in the passage of a federal law that would turn around the incentives for adoption versus foster care and that would make it financially advantageous for states to place children in adoptive homes and that would provide incentives for people to adopt children. In the past, the law provided incentives to warehouse children or to shuttle them from foster home to foster home. This is one of the laws scheduled for demolition right now, and we are going to have to start over again. Past experience teaches that the states are not likely to provide adoption incentives.

Most parents will continue to work outside the home. The nature of work in our society has changed. There was a time when we were farmers, and children saw both of their parents working. Both parents have always worked in our society. During one brief period, middle-class women thought they would be accused of being neurotic if they wanted to work. Indeed, at one point—as Dr. Steele pointed out—if a middle-aged woman wanted a career, that was prima facie evidence of neurosis. We are over that, fortunately.

As Mr. Conrad observed earlier, we must have a surrogate system of care that works—not warehousing, not the kind of day care that is so common nowadays. Day care, used as a place for diagnosis for health services, for adequate nutrition, and for thoughtful education, could be a preventive activity. Universal day care need not be a warehousing, and a comprehensive day-care program would prevent delinquency by preventing bad or inadequate socialization.

It is nonsense to insist that all mothers stay home to take care of the child and live only on Aid to Families with Dependent Children (A.F.D.C.). Current day care in the United States, however, is for the most part awful. We can, nonetheless, make it better with some fairly simple changes. For example, day care usually pays minimum wages. I went through an enormous battle in one Georgia county while setting up the child-care system of the Appalachia Regional Commission. They wanted to pay the child-care workers the minimum wage, to ensure that anytime the mill needed people, they could be gotten from the day-care centers and the nursery schools. Mill work was obviously valued more highly than was continuity of care for the children.

Paying people is not enough. There must be enough service to provide for adequate socialization, an investment we have not been willing to make. But, as Dr. Steele suggests, it is one that will not cost very much. For example, if we have a universal service system, as Singapore does, one of the tasks young people could do during the time they paid their dues for being in the society would be to work with children.

The institutions of society must also provide the same socialization lesson as the home. Unfortunately, we have done a magnificent job in the last thirty years of separating the school from the home, and the home from the world of work. There used to be a pretty good connection among those institutions. A child would come home from school with homework, through which his parents monitored what was happening in school. Indeed, particularly for fathers, homework was a way to participate in the child's education. Further, the involvement of parents reinforced the value of educational activity in the child's mind. This presented a point of concordance between home and school that we no longer have. Consolidation of the rural school began the end of that process. Homework and parental visits to the school are disappearing from the community. For example, the current Washington, D.C. teachers'-union contract provides that teachers need to see parents only twice a year, and then only during the open-house evenings.

Separation of the home from the school comes at a time when we are more aware than ever before of the importance of the home—and its values—in academic achievement. We have created an enormous gap between these two institutions, but we can close it, if we choose.

A caring adult is not enough if the schools are promoting values and demands that conflict with the values of the home. Unfortunately, we often have a tyranny of the majority rather than respect for pluralism in our society. The bilingual-education program, a good, current example of such a distortion, started out with the intent of respecting cultures but became a tool for permanent isolation of Hispanic children from the mainstream of our society. In the bilingual-education movement, a perfectly good idea was interpreted to the point of negative utility.

We know that residential institutions are not good agents of socialization. Residential group care of children has grave limitations and should be reserved for those kids for whom there is no other option and only for periods as infrequent and as brief as possible. On the other hand, keeping a child at home at any cost is ludicrous. No one—neither mother nor child—should be trapped in an abusive home. Only lately has our society been willing to protect people who are being dangerously treated in the home. The rights of families do not include the right to destroy people.

Briefly, six kinds of preventive activities as follows suggested themselves in light of Dr. Steele's observations:

First, we must ensure people the opportunity to make informed choices of parenthood, with alternatives freely available.

Second, we need a system of guaranteeing that people at a very early age begin to learn about the responsibilities and joys of parenthood.

Third, we need a system assuring continuity of care, both in the home and in child-care institutions.

Fourth, we need an articulation of the home and school, so that the learnings that a child gets from each match up in some sensible way.

Fifth, we need an articulation of home and work so that children begin to understand the meaning of work from an early age.

Sixth and finally, there must be a clear pay-off to the child for successful socialization; being a good kid ought to have real rewards.

Although these kinds of activities do have costs, they are more economical—in the long run—than are remedial programs.

Roundtable

Steele: Day care can be terrible for children, or it can be absolutely wonderful. It can be very beneficial for abused children. We have for several years run a therapeutic preschool for physically or obviously neglected kids of two to about five years old. Many of these children are depressed, have poor language development, are fearful or upset, and in all sorts of ways are unable to play. Some are hyperactive, quite aggressive, or destructive. Often, after only six months, and certainly after about a year, the majority of these children are turned around, have learned to enjoy life, to play well, and to trust some adults. Their learning and language development has improved enormously, and almost all of these children can be mainstreamed into the regular school system. This means a tremendous savings later on, not only in money (because special education will not be required and deliquency will be prevented), but in terms of prevention of human misery. Many learning problems are quite remediable if discovered and treated early. In that sense, day care can be one of the most useful preventive measures, and it is not too difficult to set up.

The intervention, however, should be early. By two years of age, and certainly by three, patterns are well set in children. The expression of violence is learned very early in life.

Scott: In your consideration of child abuse, Dr. Steele, do you get beyond the family? Others, such as teachers, police, or peers can be abusive. The neighborhoods in many places are combat zones. What are the consequences to children growing up in this almost totally abusive environment?

Steele: Not all children growing up in this environment become aggressive or delinquent. Some studies reflect inner-city patterns of delinquency and abuse almost identical with the semirural community I referred to earlier. The one common denominator is what goes on between parents and children long before society becomes involved. Babies do not spend their first year or two on the street. Before they get into the general culture, children have learned their troubles or have learned about care, empathy, and love. The environment the child experiences within the family is the more primary and the more effective.

New York's Lower East side had devasting poverty and hardship during the Depression. Out of this environment, came many of our famous artists, producers, literary people, and the like. That environment was predominantly Jewish, and Jewish families manifest a deep sense of love and care for their children. Indeed, the only significant correlation between race or religion and child abuse is a low incidence of such abuse in the Jewish population that, despite enormous difficulties, managed a good deal of excellent, loving child care.

Gilman: Much the same could be said of Harlem in the 1920s and 1930s, which produced many talented artists. The crucial factor is either God or magic, but it is the essential nature of the human spirit to rise above the most oppressive conditions. Perhaps to eliminate the problem will eliminate the very situation that gives our society energy and creativity. One must sometimes take the bitter with the sweet, and maybe delinquency and crime are the price we pay for the other things we enjoy.

Hopson: When parents are not violent toward the child but lack love and empathy (that is, where you have neglect without abuse), is the situation different?

Steele: Not much different. What causes the trouble is rarely the bruising of the child but rather the fact that the bruising was caused by somebody the child looks to for protection and love. People who have not been cared for do not care for other people. All of us have the ability to be aggressive, but what keeps us from exercising that ability is the capacity for love and empathy.

Nevertheless, one trying to persuade a court or legislature to take action can make more headway talking about physically abused and battered children through the use of pictures and the like.

Chinlund: The situation of the child after three years of age is not really hopeless. There are many effective methods of intervention, and the fact that they are not being used has to do not with the state of the art but rather with the state of our resolve to use them.

Steele: In therapy, social casework, behavior modification, the Big Brother Program, or whatever, the most important background factor is the presence of a caring figure—whether a grandmother, an aunt, a nice lady next door, a minister, school counselor, a Big Brother, or *somebody*. With such a caring figure, the outlook for almost any form of treatment is much better.

Chinlund: The sociopath, as an untreatable person, is a myth. He would not be breathing if he did not know somebody loved him enough for him to go on bothering to live. With positive peer culture properly set up, the chances of his responding are excellent. That has been documented.

Lazar: My colleagues and I are presently studying a fairly large group of people who made it out of the ghettos and into the middle- and upper-middle-class culture. What these people had in common was a great deal of overt affection from a very strong and caring parent, but a parent who made considerable demands with regard to achievement. They also had a break—but just one.

Gilman: My fear is that schools will teach parenting the way they teach sex education, eliminating anything about affection, emotion, or love. I am not sure we should trust something as sensitive to the state educational system.

Also, why is the issue whether women should work or not, or give up the children to child care or not? Why shouldn't the father play a role in bringing up the child?

Stroud: I spoke with a client while he was under a sentence of death. He had been placed in Central State Hospital at age thirteen for raping and brutally attacking a woman. He was put into a foster home after about a year. Despite a very caring foster family, he ended up convicted of murder and sentenced to death. He once remarked to me, "Well, if they had just got me when I was eight." I do not know why he picked the age of eight, but if they had gotten to him earlier, perhaps something could have been done.

Steele: The techniques and mechanics of parenting can perhaps be taught in junior high school; I do not believe junior high can provide the basic empathic ability needed for good care. This must be learned early in life and can be learned even from formerly abusive parents. I worked with parents who had badly beaten up two little kids; those parents now operate a licensed foster home for particularly difficult kids. To do our therapeutic job, we must make people having difficulties feel that it is safe to ask for help. We must establish lifelines.

**Part V
Legal and Constitutional
Problems of Intervention**

7

The Legal and Constitutional Context of Delinquency Intervention: A History

David Gilman

The authority of the state to intervene in the lives of children considered to be at risk and the legal restraints on its exercise constitute, in fact, a story of the development of the juvenile-court system. Any analysis of constitutional or legal restraints in this area must be viewed within the context of the court's purpose, goals, and structure.

Beginning in the mid-nineteenth century, child-welfare advocates were concerned with the rapid increase in street crime and the dismal condition of urban industrial life, especially insofar as it affected children. Urging formation of a new social philosophy, child-welfare advocates proposed a socialized juvenile-court system committed to providing deviant or wayward youth with the treatment, discipline, and control necessary for a law-abiding life. They argued that children did not benefit from the then-existing criminal-court process. Exposing children to adult offenders only increased the children's vulnerability and propensity toward criminality.

Reformers claimed that criminal courts were punitively based on the premises of deterrence and incapacitation. Children, they said, were not little adults; their lack of maturity diminished their capacity for being responsible for their actions. The criminal process with its punitive orientation, its legislative structure, and its adversarial nature was inappropriate to the needs of children. Child-welfare advocates, influenced in part by the emerging theories of social work and Freudian psychology, claimed that the traditional criminal-court model was inappropriate and pressed for a totally different response to juvenile deviant behavior.

The juvenile court was based in part on the assumption that children, because of their lack of maturity and their diminished mental capacity, should not be subject to adult criminal standards. The court's purpose would not be punishment, retribution, or deterrence but rather treatment and rehabilitation. This approach to intervention, substituting informal civil process for a criminal forum, was lynchpinned on the social theory that the causes of juvenile delinquency were both identifiable and susceptible to treatment. As stated at the 1886 meeting of the National Conference of Charities and Corrections, ''When the individual enters upon a criminal career, let us try to catch him at a tender age and subject him to rational social discipline such as is already successful in enough cases to show that it might be greatly extended."[1]

Juvenile-court proponents believed that juvenile delinquency was caused by either environmental neglect (for example, poverty or family instability), by individual pathology, or by a combination of these factors. If delinquency is merely symptomatic of an underlying illness, the reasoning went, then the juvenile court should espouse a medical rather than a punitive-justice model. Treatment services for children should be championed, and the full procedural and substantive rights afforded adult offenders were deemed irrelevant in a court designed to act in the child's best interest. The court, it was claimed, should determine whether the child is at risk or in need of services and care, rather than whether the child is legally responsible for the commission of a specific crime. Rather than emphasizing the child's responsibility for a criminal act, the court should speak of pathology, illness, and environmental neglect. In short, the emphasis was placed not on what the child did, but rather what the child needed, and the act only triggered state intervention to effect positive change in behavior.

Given the premise that juveniles who commit crime should be treated as irresponsible, sick persons, legal formalistic procedures became not only irrelevant, but an obstacle, and the judge, in order to evaluate properly the child's need for services, required detailed psychological and social-history reports. As stated in a 1925 publication, "The Chancery Procedure in the Juvenile Court":[2] "We cannot know the child without a thorough examination. We must have not merely the heredity, not merely the environment; we must have the physical, mental and the psychological makeup of the child. . . . We must reach into the soul-life of the child."[3]

Treatment of delinquent youth deemed to be suffering from environmental neglect often required their removal from home or community. Children who had not committed a crime but who were considered to exhibit antisocial tendencies were labeled as predelinquents and destined for a life of criminality unless the state was able to intervene. Thus, status offenders consisting of runaways, truants, or incorrigibles were included in the court's jurisdiction.

In "Procedure of the Boston Juvenile Court," cited in Platt's, *The Child Savers*,[4] it is said:

> The Court does not confine its attention to just the particular offense which brought the child to its notice. For example, a boy who comes to Court for some small such trifle as failing to wear his badge when selling papers may be held on probation for months because of difficulties at school, and a boy who comes in for playing ball on the street may . . . be committed to a reform school because he is found to have habits of loafing, stealing or gambling which cannot be corrected outside.[5]

Thus, in the early years of the juvenile court, its procedures were remarkably informal. Lawyers were not assigned to represent the child or parents. Rather, a probation officer, an employee of the court, represented the child. There was no notice of the charges, no established procedure for examining witnesses or documents, no opportunity to prepare a defense. Pretrial procedures, such as grand-jury indictments and suppression proceedings, were absent. Often, the adjudication process and the dispositional hearing were merged. The hearings were private—ostensibly to protect the vulnerable youth—and jury trials were forbidden.

This socialized juvenile court was grounded on three principles: parens patriae, individual justice, and the child's treatment needs. Parens patriae, an English Common Law doctrine adopted by the juvenile court as the basis for the assumption of jurisdiction over children, allows the state to exercise authority usually reserved for parents on a determination that the child is not receiving proper parental guidance or care and requires the protection of the state. When applied to children found to be in need of treatment for rehabilitative services, the doctrine is considered justification for the physical removal of children from the parental home. The doctrine places the state in the position of determining whether the child is receiving adequate parental care and protection without committing the state to establish exact standards for measuring appropriate parental care.

Having thus established a basis for exercising state authority over children, the juvenile court next embraced individualized justice, a concept fundamental to the implementation of the court's rehabilitative purpose. The appropriate disposition of a child deemed to have committed a delinquent act would depend on the child's needs, and the determination of his needs would require an individual assessment of the child's personal history and family situation. This requires the state to undertake a detailed social-history investigation. If a disposition is designed to treat rather than punish, in short, how can the court order proper treatment without being informed of the individual needs of the child?

These social-history reports have traditionally played a dominant role in dispositional hearings. In their reliance on social history in fashioning proper individual rehabilitative dispositions, the juvenile courts have more in common with therapeutic civil commitments. Because individuals respond to treatment differently, civil commitments are usually indefinite in duration, release being determined not by time, but rather by the progress made by the patient. The juvenile-court law conceptually falls somewhere between civil and criminal commitment law because, although an individualized disposition may be for an indeterminate period of time in order to assess the child's responsiveness to treatment, the court cannot exert its authority after the child has attained its majority.

The third guiding principle is the child's "best interests" or need for treatment. More often than not, the only guidance or standard provided the juvenile-court judge for selecting a particular disposition, this vague, broad, and undefinable concept has been said to have resulted in grossly disparate dispositions and unconscionable and unbridled exercise of judicial discretion. By maintaining the concept of the child's best interests as the lynchpin of dispositional choice, however, the court retained its benevolent character, its civil orientation, and its broad discretionary authority. Because best interests is incapable of uniform and specific definition, juvenile-court dispositional orders have been historically insulated from normal judicial review. In short, as originally envisioned, the juvenile court has been the forum for asserting control over the life of the child requiring treatment, supervision, or protection. The court is a true hybrid, having both civil commitment and criminal-model aspects. Deviant or antisocial behavior is required for adjudication. Need for treatment or services is the major factor determining disposition. The nonadversarial process of adjudication was designed for informal application. The court, in both function and design, was a marriage between psychological theory and social-work principles, housed in a legalistic structure called a juvenile court.

During the early 1900s, most states were quick to adopt the juvenile-court model, some extending the concept to encompass the entire panoply of family matters. About four states include within the family-court jurisdiction not only traditional juvenile-court cases but issues such as custody, divorce, annulment, separation, and intrafamily offenses. In both the juvenile- and family-court models, however, the characterizing philosophy is similar.

1. Children, because of their age and lack of maturity, should be less strictly accountable for their behavior than adults.
2. The primary objective of the juvenile-justice system is to provide services and treatment for deviant juvenile behavior in order to help juveniles develop and mature properly.
3. Dispositions should be based on the individual needs of each offender and should be in the child's best interests.
4. The court, in order to fulfill these objectives, must have procedures that are flexible, informal, and nonadversarial.

Critics of the juvenile-justice system argued that juveniles labeled "delinquents" and incarcerated in institutions for treatment are indistinguishable from criminal-court offenders, except that juveniles are not afforded constitutional due process. If an adult subject to criminal-law sanctions is granted full due-process protections, then surely a juvenile needs even more protection from arbitrary denials of liberty.

In 1966, the U.S. Supreme Court, in *Kent* vs. *United States*,[6] expressed its concern by recognizing the need for constitutional standards in juvenile-court proceedings. The Court concluded that the juvenile-court process might do children more harm than good.

> While there can be no doubt of the original laudable purpose of juvenile courts, studies and critiques in recent years raise serious questions as to whether actual performance measures well enough against theoretical purpose to make tolerable the immunity of the process from the reach of constitutional guarantees applicable to adults. . . .There is evidence, in fact, that there may be grounds for concern that the child receives the worst of both worlds: That he gets neither the protections accorded to adults nor the solicitous care and regenerative treatment postulated for children.[7]

In re Gault,[8] decided the following year, firmly established the right of delinquent children to due process. The Court held it unconstitutional to adjudicate juvenile delinquents without providing notice of the charges, the right to counsel, the rights of confrontation and cross-examination of sworn witnesses, and the privilege against self-incrimination. Speaking for the majority, Justice Fortas put the constitutional issues in perspective: "Neither the Fourteenth Amendment nor the Bill of Rights is for adults alone."[9]

The Challenge of Crime in a Free Society,[10] the 1967 report of the President's Commission on Law Enforcement and Administration of Justice, reflected executive interest in juvenile justice and expressed concern with both the procedures and philosophy of the juvenile-justice system.

> Studies conducted by the Commission, legislative inquiries in various states, and reports by informed observers compel the conclusion that the great hopes originally held for the juvenile court have not been fulfilled. It has not succeeded significantly in rehabilitating delinquent youth, in reducing or even stemming the tide of delinquency, or in bringing justice and compassion to the child offender.[11]

The U.S. Supreme Court, subsequently expanding the constitutional protections for juveniles, held, in *In re Winship*,[12] that delinquency proceedings require a beyond a reasonable doubt standard of proof when the delinquent act at issue would be a crime if committed by an adult.

Yet the Court was not prepared to apply to juvenile-court procedures the full panoply of adult constitutional protections. In 1971, the Court held, in *McKeiver* v. *Pennsylvania*,[13] that juveniles do not have a constitutional right to trial by jury. The majority suggested that the juvenile system must be afforded time to develop a means of accommodating both the individual's interest in constitutional protection and the state's interest in its role as parens patriae.

The juvenile concept held high promise. We are reluctant to say that, despite disappointments of grave dimensions, it still does not hold promise, and we are particularly reluctant to say that the system cannot accomplish its rehabilitative goals. We are reluctant to disallow the states to experiment further and to seek in new and different ways the elusive answers to the problems of the young, and we feel that we would be impeding that experimentation by imposing the jury trial.[14]

These landmark decisions have had a profound impact on the juvenile court. Many believed that *Gault* heralded the destruction of the court as a unique social institution, claiming that fundamental fairness and due-process guarantees represented the demise of the parens patriae court in favor of an adversary model that was inappropriate to the court's goals and purposes. In the decade after *Gault*, many court decisions expanded the notion of due process by applying in various degrees the rules of criminal procedure to juvenile-court adjudications.[15]

Constitutionally mandated counsel in delinquency cases have pushed hard to secure the fullest possible range of due-process protections for their clients. These efforts have resulted in an expansion of procedural due process from initial arrest through the adjudication hearing. Except for grand-jury indictments, bail, jury trials, and public hearings, a delinquency proceeding is almost procedurally identical to an adult-criminal trial. Indeed, this formalized procedure is being codified by statute in many states.

Although the due-process revolution in delinquency cases has substituted an adversarial process for an informal, flexible, fact-finding hearing, the heart and soul of the juvenile court—namely, its broad powers over disposition—remains unimpaired. Indeterminate sentences for treatment, parole for those considered cured, and removal of children from their parental home for treatment also remain unaffected.

This does not minimize the impact of the due-process revolution. Many a state, for instance, has redefined delinquency more narrowly to apply only to violations of its penal code. Other juvenile misconduct has been redefined under the new category of "person in need of supervision" (PINS). In many states, counsel is routinely appointed, and pleadings, discovery, and motion practice have been codified into newly revised juvenile codes. Nonetheless, not until the mid-1970s was there a concerted effort to suggest an alternative model for delinquency dispositions.

The IJA-ABA (Institute of Judicial Administration-American Bar Association) Juvenile Justice Standards,[16] representing a substantial departure from both the philosophical premises and the unbridled judicial discretion of traditional delinquency dispositions, offer a radically different approach to dispositions, reject the treatment or medical model, and represent a decade-long effort to develop national uniform standards for the entire juvenile-justice system. Although the standards cover the full panoply of juvenile-justice issues, only those affecting the purpose and goals of delinquency dispositions will be reviewed here.

Many state juvenile codes allow removal from the home if a juvenile "needs treatment" or if confinement would be in the juvenile's best interest. The juvenile court, however, has often placed these children in secure facilities more resembling prisons than hospitals or schools. Institutionalization, in the view of the standards, is inherently coercive and antithetical to legitimate treatment goals. The standards recognize, however, that some juveniles are serious threats to the community. Institutionalization may be the only appropriate disposition for some of them. In such cases, confinement should not be justified on rehabilitative grounds, but on traditional criminal-law factors, such as the offender's age, seriousness of the offense, prior record, and aggravating and mitigating circumstances surrounding the commission of the act. These dispositional factors can be objectively measured and fairly evaluated. On the other hand, a subjective judgment concerning a juvenile's need for treatment and the ability to function in society, if released, required predictions of future behavior that cannot be reliably assessed.

Under the standards, a sentence of a juvenile to secure placement for a serious felony cannot be shortened or lengthened based on the juvenile's participation or lack of participation in a treatment program. The standards reject coercive treatment in secure placement as an impermissible invasion of the juvenile's privacy and liberty interests. Furthermore, treatment in such a setting is usually ineffective.

If the judge sentences a juvenile to a nonsecure facility or to probation, treatment needs are a legitimate sentencing factor. Reflecting disillusionment with the treatment ideal, the standards concluded that the opportunity for effective treatment is enhanced in a less coercive and more open setting.

In the traditional juvenile-court system, social history played the dominant role in sentencing. But social histories have been characterized as unreliable, vague, and subjective. Since many, if not most, delinquents suffer from some degree of environmental and family neglect, the present system allows incarceration for treatment purposes for almost any delinquent act. Indeed, a disproportionate number of children placed in secure facilities have never been adjudicated guilty of a serious crime but instead were found to be "in need of services."

The cornerstone of the standards' sentencing scheme is that all sentences—regardless of their severity—must be determinate. Maximum sentences, based on the principle of proportionality, must be fixed by the legislature. Under the standards, the court fixes the severity of the sentence and length of stay within the legislatively determined maximum.

For example, if a crime is serious enough to warrant a maximum sentence of three years of secure confinement, the sentencing judge may sentence the juvenile up to the maximum or give a less severe sanction. If the juvenile is a first offender, if mitigating circumstances attend the act, or if the juvenile is of a very young age, the sentence may be decreased. The judge retains the discretion to incarcerate or not, to make the sentence severe (up to the legislative maximum in secure confinement), or to order a less drastic sentence (probation or nonsecure confinement), if permissible factors so warrant. The judge must give reasons for whatever sentence is imposed and state why less severe sanctions were considered and rejected.

Irrespective of the seriousness of the crime, the standards oppose mandatory sentences. The judge, instead, is provided with the flexibility to fashion an appropriate sentence within the legislatively established maximums. In addition, all sentences must be determinate so that the juvenile, the public, and the victim know what the sentence is and how long it will be enforced. Sentencing decisions thus remain with the judiciary rather than being delegated to correctional personnel or program personnel.

The standards' support for determinate sentences is the logical consequence of rejecting treatment goals as a legitimate basis for institutionalization. Once the punitive nature of juvenile sentences is acknowledged, it follows that sentences must be limited in duration and severity to sustain the fundamental fairness of the disposition. In determining severity and duration of a disposition, treatment becomes a secondary consideration.

Determinate sentences do not mean that rehabilitative services cannot be made available to incarcerated delinquents. The standards emphasize, however, that participation in treatment programs cannot be coerced by threats of lengthened incarceration, or promises of early release.

The standards, by their very nature, do not carry the weight of court decision, but they are persuasive in legislative-code revision efforts and tend to provide, at the very least, food for profitable thought. The standards directly challenge the premises and assumptions of traditional juvenile-court dispositional authority and raise serious questions concerning the rationale for state intervention. In a more direct way, the formalization and procedural mandates of due process, when combined with the standards' recommendations concerning dispositional discretion, raise the more fundamental question of whether a specialized court for delinquency is still viable. These issues and their implications must be addressed by those interested in the future of the juvenile-justice system.

Notes

1. National Conference of Charities and Corrections, *"Nature* v. *Nature* in the Making of Social Careers", in *Proceedings of the National Conference of Charities and Corrections* (Grand Rapids, Mich.: National Conference of Charities and Corrections, 1896).

2. J. Mack, "The Chancery Procedure in the Juvenile Court," in *The Child, the Clinic and the Court* (New York: New Republic, 1925).

3. Ibid., p. 315.

4. "Procedure of the Boston Juvenile Court," *Survey* 23 (February 1910):649, cited in A. Platt, *The Child Savers* (Chicago: University of Chicago, 1969), p. 142.

5. Ibid.

6. *Kent v. United States,* 383 U.S. 541 (1966).

7. Ibid., pp. 555-556.

8. *In re Gault,* 387 U.S. 1 (1967).

9. Ibid., p. 13.

10. President's Commission on Law Enforcement and Administration of Justice, *The Challenge of Crime in a Free Society* (Washington, D.C.: U.S. Government Printing Office, 1967).

11. Ibid., p. 80.

12. *In re Winship*, 397 U.S. 358 (1970).

13. *McKeiver v. Pennsylvania,* 403 U.S. 528 (1971).

14. Ibid., p. 547.

15. See *Breed v. Jones,* 421 U.S. 519 (1975); *Gesicki v. Oswald,* 336 F. Supp. 371 (S.D.N.Y. 1971); *DeBacker v. Braenard,* 396 U.S. 28 (1969); *Harris v. New York*, 401 U.S. 222 (1971); *Ivan v. City of New York*, 407 U.S. 203 (1972); *Martarella v. Kelley,* 359 F. Supp. 478 (S.D.N.Y. 1973); *Morales v. Truman,* 403 U.S. 322 (1977).

16. *IJA-ABA Juvenile Justice Standards* (Cambridge, Mass.: Ballinger, 1980).

Commentary

Dan Hopson

The changes proposed by the standards, if adopted by courts or state legislatures, would raise more important and more difficult constitutional and legal issues concerning early intervention than our more traditional philosophies. To date, only the state of Washington, (and it not completely), has adopted the just-deserts approach, with proportionate sentencing and the rest.[1] Since most of our courts still approach children in more traditional terms, let us examine the question of early intervention under a more conventional legal theory.

At least three different approaches might be taken toward early childhood intervention. Each raises different issues and, from the child's point of view, two different arguments might be made.

The first approach would treat children who have been properly identified on some basis in the same manner as children needing special-education or mental-health services. Conceptually, this would involve a voluntary program, with parents being informed of the child's problem and, in theory, the community making available the necessary services. The development of the comprehensive community mental-health clinic through legislation in the 1960s is an example of this approach.[2] Under such legislation, a child labeled "mentally or emotionally ill" was referred to the clinic.

Perhaps a better example for our purposes is federal legislation granting children labeled "developmentally disabled" the right to an individual educational plan and the right to be "mainstreamed."[3] Although, because of the underlying compulsory-education law, it shades into the second approach that I will discuss later, this legislation provides a model for the children we are talking about. This voluntary-services model presents few constitutional or other legal problems. To date, courts have not been very sympathetic to the child resisting the voluntary services chosen by the parents. In *Parham*,[4] for example, the U.S. Supreme Court allowed parents "voluntarily" to commit their children to state mental hospitals, although with certain restrictions, which will be discussed by Kenneth Stroud. Presumably, therefore, the Court would allow parents to place a child in a predelinquent treatment program. Cases like *Belotti II*,[5] and *Tinker*,[6] which give children some control over their lives, based on due process, seem limited to abortion rights, free-speech rights, and the like. In any voluntary-treatment contest between the parents and the state, on the one hand, and the child on the other, the former would prevail.

Legal issues might arise, however, in connection with ordinary malpractice or equal protection. For example, a person making an incorrect diagnosis of "potential delinquent" might be held liable in damages for malpractice to a child placed in a treatment program. Proof of causation, however, in such cases would be extremely difficult. The state or a diagnostician might also be held liable in a converse situation, (for example, one involving a refusal to label the child as a potential delinquent), particularly if the services were free or subsidized. The denial of a correct labeling could similarly raise equal-protection arguments on behalf of the child denied the special services reserved for the developmentally disabled. Indeed, even children correctly labeled could argue, under equal protection, an entitlement to voluntary-service programs.[7]

A second approach involves compulsory services for the "potentially delinquent" child. There could be two different forms of coercive statutes. First would be a statute requiring treatment along the lines of compulsory vaccination,[8] compulsory quarantine for kids with measles,[9] mandatory automobile child restraints,[10] requirements that certain children have certain kinds of medicine put in their eyes at birth,[11] compulsory educational tracking statutes,[12] and the more general compulsory-education statute.[13] Statutes embodying these requirements take the decision-making right away from the parents but have all been upheld under the general concept of the state's police power. This police power is justified, in turn, on the notion that individual rights must suffer in order to protect others, like in the vaccination statutes,[14] or that an educated citizenry is a necessary part of our civilization, as in compulsory-education statutes,[15] or even on the grounds that the state, under its police power, can help an individual child.[16] These exercises of police power do not rely on the parens patriae concept of the juvenile court but on the police power to protect ourselves and to protect children in our society.

Such statutes do occasionally run into trouble. One problem involves the incorrect identification of people subject to the compulsory treatment. The Washington, D.C. educational tracking procedure was declared unconstitutional because the identification process was inefficient.[17]

Clearly, the child must be able to challenge in court whatever label is placed on him. There is, however, usually no problem in building into the statute this opportunity for challenge. There is, in the "potential delinquent" labeling process, however, an especially difficult identification problem. In special-education situations, we can use I.Q.; for quarantines, we can tell who has the measles. For compulsory education, generally, it is reasonably easy to determine the subjects by age. Early childhood intervention with regard to delinquency prevention has no such easy criterion.

Other problems loom in a compulsory service statute: equal protection or due process, First Amendment, and right-to-privacy arguments. If whatever test we apply to predict future delinquent behavior yields a disproportionate number of minority children, which is likely to be the result, the statute and its operation might be declared unconstitutional on the same basis as the tracking situation,[18] and as the special-education case in California.[19]

Likewise, the First Amendment, freedom-of-religion cases might cause a court to allow the parents to opt out of a program, just as certain parents were allowed to opt out of general compulsory education.[20] This problem, too, could be resolved by statutorily allowing for the opting out.

Whether the recently developed right to privacy[21] would cause a court to declare unconstitutional our compulsory statute—whatever form it takes—is another question. The right to privacy, possessing great emotional appeal to most of us, and used to strike down such things as criminal abortion statutes,[22] contraception laws,[23] and certain pornography statutes,[24] has not in fact been used on a constitutional level to outlaw compulsory-education laws, child-labor laws, or the like. The U.S. Supreme Court will not be as interested in using privacy concepts to strike down statutes legislatures have found necessary or helpful for protecting and benefiting children.

A third and final approach would create a new status category in the traditional juvenile court called "potential delinquent" or, as Dave Bahlmann suggests, "green giraffes." Already, states have various labels enabling the state to intervene in the life of an individual child: PINS (person in need of supervision), or CHINS (children in need of supervision), into which we can put status offenders such as neglected or dependent children and a variety of other children. These categories are traditional.

The original goal of the juvenile court was to reach out to what was then called "predelinquent" children. This was done by including within the term *delinquent* a very broad range of children, what we would call today the "status offenders." Indiana's old statute,[25] a very typical example, included children bouncing around railroad yards or truck terminals, associating with immoral people, or engaging in conduct injurious to self or others—horribly broad definitions. The Texas statute[26] included children engaged in "immoral" behavior. Nonetheless, state supreme courts have generally upheld these very broad definitions against vagueness challenges and substantive due-process challenges questioning whether the state can reach such children for compulsory treatment.[27]   The Illinois legislature made it a *crime* for a child to violate the curfew statute.[28] Reviewing that statute, the Illinois Supreme Court stated that the legislature could keep children off the street after 2:00 A.M.[29] Since there is a lot of crime, keeping children off the street after 2:00 A.M. will cut down on crime and is a perfectly legitimate legislative purpose.[30] If a legislature can punish as criminal a child who has done nothing more than be out on the street at 2:00 A.M., a fortiori green giraffes can be constitutionally treated.

Since I obviously do not like the Illinois court's decision, I offer these suggestions in connection with any individualized intervention with our green giraffes. First, our social and behavioral scientists must develop predictions that are more than 50-percent accurate. This does not, of course, preclude different criteria at different ages. Second, any such intervention procedure requires legislation with reasonably specific terms that are verifiable, so that people can testify to the meaning of the terms *green giraffe* or *potential delinquent* and, therefore, what in fact the state can do.

Caution is, of course, indicated since much evidence demonstrates the potential in the juvenile-justice system for doing great harm. Nonetheless— to the extent that we can come up with reasonably accurate predictions—false pleas of privacy, pluralism, or democracy are not very realistic. Under current constitutional doctrines, we can and should intervene. To allow a child to become an adult criminal in the name of privacy, pluralism, or democracy is unfair to that child. We need not sit by and allow the child to spend most of his life in prison on the grounds that he chose it at the age of six. Even in our fumbling way, we can do better than that.

Notes

1. Wash. Rev. Code §§ 13.40.010 et seq. (1979 Supp.).

2. Community Mental Health Centers Act, 42 U.S.C. §§ 2681 et seq. (1963).

3. Developmental Disabilities Services and Facilities Construction Amendments of 1970, 42 U.S.C. §§ 2670-2677c (1970), transferred to 42 U.S.C. §§ 6007-6008; 6061-6066 (1975).

4. *Parham* v. *J.R.,* 442 U.S. 584 (1979).

5. *Bellotti* v. *Baird,* 443 U.S. 622 (1979).

6. *Tinker* v. *Des Moines School District,* 393 U.S. 503 (1969).

7. See *Goldberg* v. *Kelley,* 397 U.S. 254 (1970).

8. See, for example, Ill. Rev. Stat. ch. 111½, ¶¶ 22.11-22b. (1979). See also *Jacobsen* v. *Commonwealth of Massachusetts,* 197 U.S. 11 (1905).

9. Ill. Rev. Stat. ch. 111½, ¶ 22 (1979); see also *People ex rel. Barmore* v. *Robertson,* 302 Ill. 422, 134 N.E. 815 (1922) (defining scope of Department of Health's power to quarantine).

10. See "History of Passive Restraint Systems," in *Report on DOT Passive Restraint Rule* (Washington, D.C.: Subcommittee on Consumer Finance and Protection, House Committee on Interstate and Foreign Commerce, 95th Congress, 1977).

11. Ill. Rev. Stat. ch. 111½, ¶ 4703 (1979).

12. See, for example, *Evans* v. *Youngblood,* 230 F. Supp. 74 (N.D. Fla. 1964); *Stell* v. *Swannah-Chatham County Board of Education,* 333 F.2d 55 (5th Cir. 1964); *Evans* v. *Ennis,* 281 F.2d 385 (3d Cir. 1960); *Miller* v. *School District No. 2 Clarendon County,* 256 F. Supp. 370 (D.S.C. 1966).

13. See Ill. Rev. Stat. ch. 122, ¶ 26-1 et seq. (1979); see also *Meyer* v. *Nebraska,* 262 U.S. 390 (1923) (upholding right of state legislatures to enact compulsory school attendance statutes, but not to prohibit the teaching of German.)

14. See note 8, *supra.*

15. Areen, "Alternative Schools: Better Guardians than Family or State?" *University of Chicago School Review* 81 (1973): 175.

16. See for example, Ill. Rev. Stat. ch. 37, ¶ 703-1 (1979) (granting police authority to take into custody a minor who the officer believes is neglected, delinquent, or " . . . found on any street or public place suffering from any sickness or injury which requires care . . . ").

17. *Hobson* v. *Hansen,* 269 F. Supp. 401 (D.D.C. 1967), *aff'd, Smuck* v. *Hansen,* 408 F.2d 175 (D.C. Cir. 1969). See also *Diana* v. *State Board of Education,* Card no. C-70-37 RFR (N.D. Cal., Feb. 5, 1970); *Larry P.* v. *Riles,* 343 F. Supp. 1306 (N.D. Cal 1972), *aff'd,* 502 F.2d 963 (9th Cir. 1974).

18. Ibid.

19. *Larry P.* v. *Riles,* 495 F. Supp. 926 (N.D. Cal. 1979).

20. *Wisconsin* v. *Yoder,* 406 U.S. 205 (1972).

21. *Griswold* v. *Connecticut,* 381 U.S. 479 (1965).

22. *Roe* v. *Wade,* 410 U.S. 113 (1973).

23. *Eisenstadt* v. *Baird,* 405 U.S. 438 (1972).

24. *Carey* v. *Population Services International,* 431 U.S. 678 (1977).

25. 1945 Ind. Acts ch. 356, § 4, now codified at Ind. Code § 31-5-7-4 (1971).

26. Tex. Rev. Civ. Stat. Ann. art. 43, § 2338-1, Sec. 3 (1971). (Repealed by 1973 Tex. Acts ch. 543, § 3, eff. Jan. 1, 1974, See, now, Tex. Fam. Code Ann. tit. 3, § 51.03 (Vernon Supp. 1981). See also *E.S.G.* v. *State,* 447 S.W.2d (Tex. Civ. App. 1969), *cert. denied,* 398 U.S. 956 (1970).

27. See, for example, *In re Patricia A.,* 31 N.Y.2d 83, 286 N.E.2d 432 (1972).

28. Ill. Rev. Stat. ch. 23, § 2371 (1979).

29. *People* v. *Chambers,* 66 Ill. 2d 36, 360 N.E.2d 55 (1977).

Commentary

Kenneth M. Stroud

A coercive intervention process aimed at an individual child must undergo a much more rigid constitutional analysis than is generally applicable to full-employent statutes and day-care centers. The analysis in the coercive situation will track the *Parham*[1] case, in which the parents and the state, acting as guardians, tried to commit their respective children and wards to mental hospitals. The children involved obtained legal assistance and brought suit, arguing a violation of procedural due process.

The first question concerns the existence of any personal-liberty interest on the part of the children. Without such an interest, the parents could just waive any parental rights, and the matter would be over. The U.S. Supreme Court found that the children had a liberty interest protected by the Fourteenth Amendment, in two respects: first, a right to be free of unneccessary physical restraint and, second, a right to be free of erroneous stigmatization (that is, erroneously labeled "mentally ill").

The second question, given a protectible interest, concerns the appropriate procedure under due process. What kind of procedure will reduce the margin of error without unduly burdening the state's function? This requires a very difficult balancing of values, values that themselves are difficult to articulate. There is no mechanical way to go about this.

In *Parham,* the Court identified the government's interest in terms of resource allocation. The state wanted its psychiatric resources to go to treatment, not to preconfinement hearings.

The parental interest was identified as the right to raise the child free of unnecessary state intervention. The Court's function was to balance these in a procedure reducing the margin of error, that is, reducing the risk of unnecessarily confining the child or erroneously stigmatizing the child, without at the same time totally destroying the state's objective as reflected in the statute.

This sort of challenge arises only when a concrete mode of intervention has appeared. The missing component in this colloquium is a concrete method of intervention. Once such a method is decided on that involves the state and is coercive, one who feels his liberty infringed will come forward to attack the statute.

This will raise additional problems, touched on by Dan Hopson and John Monahan. The state will have to specify who does the intervening, who is the subject of the intervention (that is, the child, the family, or the like) and how successful the program will be (that is, whether there is predictive success with the indicators). One cannot come in with a

50-percent correlation or with a vague correlation because, in such a case, the state's interests will not outweight the child's interests. The statute will lose. The statute will prevail if its proponents can substantiate reasonable predictive success within the *Parham* formula. Indeed, in *Parham,* the Court concluded that no particularly complex due-process hearing was needed.

Although the Court did find that Fourteenth Amendment rights were implicated—raising one flag—it went on to find sufficient a standard, traditional, medical fact-gathering procedure. All that was required was a neutral fact finder—the staff psychiatrists at the mental hospital—finding the child to be mentally ill and likely to benefit from hospitalization. This done, the child can be committed. The lesson, of course, is that procedural due process, even when held to apply, need not present a very high hurdle. Nonetheless, we must be concerned about the quality of the predictions and the nature of both the intervention and the intervenors.

In *Parham,* it must be added, the battle was between the state and the parents on the one hand and the child on the other. In the type of coercive, predelinquent intervention program contemplated in our discussions, it is much more likely that the child and parents will be one unit, allied against the state.

Two other cases are worthy of mention in their implications for our topic. In *Tarasoff,*[2] a therapist was held liable in damages for not warning a potential victim of a threat presented by the therapist's client. If our intervention model involves predictions of dangerousness, those making the predictions may be subject to similar liability even though, as the *Tarasoff* court recognized, there might be a large margin of error.

A second case of interest, currently before the U.S. Supreme Court,[3] involves predictions of dangerousness in the death-sentencing stage of a criminal trial by a licensed psychiatrist named "Dr. Death." The doctor always testifies that the person is a psychopath and will commit further acts of violence. A very large proportion of the cases in which he has testified result in the application of the death penalty.

Both of these cases arise despite the position of the American Psychiatric Association that violence cannot be accurately predicted. Indeed, the association is contemplating informal and possibly intraprofessional sanctions on people who do make such predictions. The point is, of course, that if this sort of thing cannot be done, we must not go out on a limb to attempt it. Indeed, one might end up in a no-win situation: if you claim the expertise but do not warn the victim, you are liable. If you do warn the victim, and the victim suffers anxiety or distress from the warning, you may be sued for a negligent warning. Therapists, I might add, are already involved in that whipsaw in making release decisions.

Two final crucial questions involve the criteria for determining success in the intervention. When does the intervention cease, and when have we achieved success? These present a purely legal question, one that is related to the amount of deviance we are willing to tolerate.

We have assumed that most people are law-abiding and have asked, "Why do some people kill and rob?" We could turn that around to assume that everybody is a killer and robber and ask, "How do some people avoid this antisocial conduct?"

I was impressed during the conference with the political nature of the questions. Not even the narrowest intrusion can be discussed without raising deep legal and political questions. This is true not only in discussing a reorganization of the economic system but everything else, as well. Indeed, one cannot even say what one is talking about without raising such questions. In other words, this is not merely a quibble among experts, and I am confident that none of us thought it was.

Notes

1. *Parham* v. *J.L. and J.R.,* 442 U.S. 584 (1979).
2. *Tarasoff* v. *Regents of the University of California,* 17 Cal. 3d 425, 551 P.2d 334, 131 Cal. Rptr. 14 (1976).
3. See *Estelle* v. *Smith,* 451 U.S. 454 (1981), ultimately decided on Fifth Amendment (privilege against self-incrimination) and Sixth Amendment (right to counsel) grounds.

Roundtable

Bahlmann: Reference has been made to my so-called green giraffe. In working on proposed juvenile legislation, we recognized that the concept of "delinquent" began in 1889 in an attempt to avoid branding children as "convicts" or "criminal." Eventually, of course, the term *delinquent* became more damaging to the child than *convict* or *criminal,* terms with which society was more adept at dealing. We knew that ten years from now, another commission would think a change was needed. We decided, therefore, to pick "green giraffe," leaving "yellow moose" and "strawberry cow" for subsequent commissions. In short, what is important is not the label but the capability of the system to deal with juveniles and their families.

Lazar: Unlike mental retardation, mental illness, or measles, delinquency is a condition not of the individual but of the community and of the society. I do not believe we will ever be able to predict that an individual will become delinquent, although we may say that a particular child lives in conditions not conducive to optimal development that place him in danger, not of delinquency, but of some disturbance. Because he is an upset and angry kid does not mean he will commit an antisocial act as opposed to punching a ball.

We can intervene through the traditional notion of protecting children from neglect. The definition of neglect can change with the state of the art. We define the minimum level of protection and life that a child should have and, if he is not being provided it, the state has an interest in intervening.

Hopson: If we add to the definition of neglect those children who will later become delinquent or disturbed, we must show the connection between that neglect and the new category of children.

Lazar: The present neglect statutes already cover children in danger of developing inappropriate behavior.

Commentary

Cleon H. Foust

The first constitutional question with regard to intervention concerns the Fourteenth Amendment. Is it within the police power of the state to so intervene? This sort of police-power question normally requires us to ask three questions:

1. Is there a problem?
2. Will the proposed action tend to solve that problem?
3. Does that action violate some other constitutional provision?

Some time ago, a California judge—asked to tell how he knew whether an automobile driver was engaged in wilful and wanton misconduct rather than simple negligence—said that if, when the witness described the accident, the judge wanted to throw up his hands and say, "My God, you didn't do that," the conduct was wilful and wanton. I have a similar reaction with regard to due process and police power. If my reaction is to throw up my hands and say, "My God, you are not going to do that," the proposed action is probably not within the police power.

Our discussion so far reveals several different kinds of intervention: remedial or corrective and micro and macro. Macro intervention, such as John Conrad's proposals for socioeconomic readjustment, raises no new constitutional problems but rather those we have dealt with for years with regard to social legislation.

Micro intervention, however, raises different questions, including whether—even if constitutionally we can intervene in a particular way, we want to. That policy judgment will have to be made in light of the fact that any suggestion of "behavior modification," a phrase we simply have not been able to hurdle in police-power justification, will doom the proposed action.

As one might expect, due-process requirements will increase as the gravity of the intervention increases. One type of intervention and the attendant constitutional concerns is discussed in *Parham:*[1] an investigation of procedural safeguards necessary for commitment of retarded children. Such cases minimally require an inquiry by a neutral fact finder who need not be a judge or legally trained person. Some states, however, have provided judicial hearings for such interventions.[2]

There is an analogue in property law for the sort of intervention at issue. Centuries ago the so-called bill quia timet alleged that the plaintiff feared that his property was about to be irremediably invaded and that, therefore, the court should restrain the defendant. Likewise, as John Conrad has already pointed out, status offenses trigger intervention because of the fear that absent that, more serious antisocial conduct may follow.

Finally, the constitutional and legal problems are but one part of the challenge facing us. The greater problem is whether, even if constitutionally and legally allowable, a coercive system is desirable in terms of strategy-merchantability. A completely voluntary system might be preferable.

Notes

1. *Parham* v. *J.R.,* 442 U.S. 584, 1979.
2. See, e.g., N.M. Stat. Ann § 43-1-16.1 (1979).

Roundtable

Schweinhart: I must reiterate that a program need not be aimed at delinquency prevention in order to prevent delinquency but can serve multiple purposes. Indeed, I get very nervous considering the possibility of labeling three- and four-year-olds.

Hopson: Constitutionally, however, the U.S. Supreme Court may invalidate a program on due-process grounds if "X" is the program's asserted reason, but "Y" is the real purpose.

Stroud: Constitutional problems are especially likely if racial disparity is a factor. Of course, if the state is appropriately seeking to do one thing, the fact that it does other things as well will not necessarily invalidate the program.

I would ask Dr. Steele if the child-abuse correlate to delinquency is persuasive enough to justify state intervention.

Steele: Were I asked in court whether this abused child will become delinquent, I would respond, "I do not know." But if I were asked if the child shows any developmental delays, I would say, "Yes," and list them. If I were then asked if these developmental problems were remediable, I would answer "Yes," and cite the ample evidence for that proposition. If I were then asked whether without intervention the situation would improve under the present circumstance of the child's life, I would say that our experience indicates not.

In short, I would talk about the child's hampered development—social, emotional, and cognitive. Children with such hampered development may develop delinquency, but that need not be brought out.

Lazar: We must ask, however, not only whether an intervention procedure will help but whether it will hurt. In the area of personality and social behavior, we know more about what hurts than what helps. We know that labels hurt. For example, some people in the 1950s could not get jobs in defense plants because someone had written "delinquent" or some other such helpful phrase in their school records.

Hopson: Dr. Steele, under current law, a court would not have jurisdiction to take the child about whom you testified. The legislature would first have to provide a statutory basis.

Moreover, even if you testify about the future effects of nontreatment on the child, I, as parent, can still decide whether to have the treatment—at least absent a life-threatening situation or, maybe, one involving protection from future crime.

Steele: The judges before whom I have testified have used their own discretion. It is illegal to deprive a child of proper care and protection.

Bahlmann: Some courts would expand their definition of neglect to include the situation under discussion.

Gilman: Regardless of what it is called, a judicial process will probably lead to more harm that good, as our experience with the juvenile court substantiates. To be sure, some individuals improve after going through the process, but one does not know if they have been helped because of or in spite of the process. If the intervention is nonjudicial, and therefore noncoercive, do we have the political consensus that will provide the needed services (for example, the good alternative to that bad home)? After all of the defining, adjudicating, and the like, when we come to the superhighway, we still end up in the cow path; ultimately we do not know what to do. We end up with a status offender, a delinquent child, a mentally ill child, and a retarded child all sharing the same cell in the same institution receiving "treatment" about which, in terms of the effectiveness, the treaters themselves have doubts, and the kids certainly know that.

Conrad: We must recall, however, that for many conditions we simply have no remedy.

Part VI
Preventive Strategies and
Techniques

8 Preventing Juvenile Delinquency through Provision of Family-Support Services

Jan McCarthy

To set the stage, it is important to note that the ideas presented in this chapter are based on motivational theory. Acknowledging that life experiences determine the motives that evolve in the particular life-style of each child points to the need for concern about the atmosphere in which the child is reared. A child's perception, whether accurate or faulty, affects his behavior. As the child confirms his attitudes, views of life become increasingly difficult to change. Therefore, understanding the early years as well as recognizing the importance of family as the first environmental setting for the child has implications for the colloquium postulate, "discovery of and early intervention into the lives of children and families at risk can reduce later delinquency and crime."

Early childhood educators, psychologists, and others who have studied young children have devoted much attention and discussion toward the effect of intervention programs. Intelligence—socially meaningful, potentially, to both low-socioeconomic-status children and those having handicapping conditions—has dominated the research related to young children during the past two decades. Only recently have we begun to receive feedback regarding the long-term effects of programs for young children. Studies in 1978 by Weikart[1] and Lazar[2] provide solid evidence that preschool for children from low-income families affects school achievement, grade placement, and motivation, causes a reduction in placement in special-education classes, and gives parents hope that their children will succeed.

No single period of life is the *only* important stage in a child's development. Development begins in the prenatal stage and continues throughout life. Moreover, no particular life periods should be ignored or labeled insignificant. Compared to a child's school years (ages five to eighteen), the early childhood period (prenatal to age four) has been largely ignored, at least in terms of providing developmental services to the children and their families.

A large body of evidence shows that the first four years of life are especially critical in the development of language, curiosity, and social skills as well as the roots of intelligence.[3] Furthermore, Bloom conservatively estimates that the lack of nurturance could make a difference between a productive life or an institutionalized life for the individual with limited potential or the difference between a professional career and a semiskilled occupation for the individual with average potential. The first four years are also distinguished in another manner; at *no* other time will a person develop or learn as rapidly.

An examination of the child's accomplishments during the first four years is useful to the search for clues about what leads some children to delinquency at an early point in their lives. During this period, a child acquires the ability to understand the majority of the language used in ordinary conversation throughout life, develops the ability to use language as a communicative skill and a fairly stabilized personality, learns thousands of things that can or cannot be done, learns to read the mood of caregivers and to respond accordingly, and develops curiosity and interest in exploration and learning. Though a compelling desire to learn and explore is present in almost all young children, it can easily be dulled or stamped out. Young children need the opportunity to experience the success that nurtures a positive self-concept and the desire to set goals for oneself. Not to be overlooked is the impact of inconsistent expectations on how the young child learns to read the moods of others. The ability to relate to others is deeply rooted in the early years. The child's exposure to others through play experiences or attendance in a preschool provides an opportunity for peer relationships to begin to develop. These relationships are the beginnings of social roles expected by society. Nurturance of the young child is crucial whether that nurturance is provided by the family, other significant individuals in the child's life, or institutions that provide support services to families.

Regardless of the type of family constellation, the family is the primary influence during the first four years, when development is occurring at a rate unequaled in later years. The family acts as a system for delivering developmental stimulation and support that will critically influence the child's life. Strong families may be able to fulfill responsibilities with minimal outside support; however, the stresses that many families suffer limit their potential for meeting the needs of their children.

Stresses that make the family very vulnerable are created by a number of factors. Poverty is identified as one of the most deleterious conditions. Insufficient child development occurs in numerous low-income families. These inadequacies include a poor diet, inadequate health care, crowded and noisy housing, a low level of education among parents (which often means low expectations for children), a general lack of books and toys in the home (which denies children the opportunity to learn through exploration), and little emphasis on nurturing language development, curiosity, problem solving, or encouragement of the child's self-confidence.

Additionally, the incidence of *reported* child abuse and neglect, highly concentrated in the lower socioeconomic groups, is often associated with the economic and environmental stress experienced by the poor with regard to unemployment, insufficient income, inadequate and crowded housing, social isolation, lack of knowledge of parenting skills, alcohol and drug abuse, nonsupportive marital relationships, low self-esteem, and parental history of having been abused as a child. Regardless of the cause of abuse, the abused child's opportunity for developing goals and values that lead to a constructive life-style is weakened.

Another factor that places stress on the family and interferes with the parental ability to provide the nurturance a child needs involves the dynamics of American families. Because of the increase in rates of divorce and of unwed mothers who keep their children, the percentage of children under six years of age living in single-parent families has increased significantly in recent years. Although many single parents provide excellent care, support, and shelter for their children, the level of economic deprivation in a large number of single-parent, female-headed households (especially among minority families) makes adequate care difficult.

The median family income in 1978 was $17,640. For black families, the median income was $10,880 and for families of Hispanic origin $12,570. However, approximately 24.5 million persons (11.4 percent of the population) fell below the 1978 poverty level of $6,662 for a nonfarm family of four. Of black and Hispanic families, 27.5 percent and 20.4 percent, respectively, were below the poverty level.[4]

In 1979, 6 million mothers with 7.2 million preschool children were working because of economic need. Nearly two-thirds of these women were single, widowed, divorced, or separated, or had husbands whose earnings were less than $10,000.[5] Society has shown little concern about what happens to these children. Tradition is very strong. Although many people maintain that children should be cared for at home by their own mothers, some of these same people feel that more people must be moved off welfare rolls into a productive, self-supporting way of life—a paradoxical situation. With the visible participation of women in the labor force, the issue of mothers staying home has become academic; the relevant question now concerns what types of care can be made available for the millions of children involved and their families who need it.

Of major significance and perhaps great social consequence is the lack of support for those single adults responsible for maintaining a family. Adults need assistance in coping with the constant pressures of a job (or seeking and retaining a job that will adequately maintain the family), in managing the home, and in responding to the many needs of the children. With no one to share the responsibilities or assist in making decisions on troublesome matters, the burden can become too overwhelming for one individual. When frustration or despair takes over, little energy is devoted to guiding children—the role that society assumes parents will play.

Problems that interfere with a family's ability to meet the developmental needs of its children are complex. The social indicators usually provided by the Department of Health and Human Services and the Bureau of Labor Statistics provide an important but incomplete factual picture. If the family is described as an open structure—interactive with other institutions and individuals in the environment—then problems cannot be accurately described in isolation. Programs implemented to respond to one need must be examined in terms of consequences to the total family; for example, do assistance programs discourage maintaining the family unit? Care must be exerted to study the interdependence of a wide range of needs and of actions taken in response to identified needs.

At the same time, not to be overlooked is the fact that each child is a unique individual with unique abilities, interests, thoughts, and desires. Programs should nurture those individual differences and at the same time recognize that the child is part of a family. Families are the primary socializing agent of the child, and it is essential that the parents remain the most important adult figures in the child's life, even though another caregiver or a teacher may play an important role (providing the support, protection, stimulation, and guidance needed when parents cannot be present to do so).

Options in child-care arrangements should be available so that working parents might select the best for their child, whether it be in a day-care center, in a family day-care home, or in the child's own home. The need for adequate day care is pressing. According to the best available data[6] fewer than one-seventh of the 7.2 million children under six having working parents are being served in day-care centers. Those being served in centers are primarily the three- and four-year-olds. Few center-care services are available for infants and toddlers, the handicapped, and school-aged children. Although these are all very vulnerable groups, the parents of such children have few opportunities for seeking the best arrangement and have few choices for finding a match among their values, their child's needs, and the type of nurturing provided.

It is remarkably evident that the family, regardless of how it is constituted, influences—positively or negatively—the continuous development of the child. Therefore, examining qualities that have been identified as characteristics of strong families could provide positive components of any plan for supporting children and families. According to Stinnett,[7] strong families show appreciation among their members, spend time together and genuinely enjoy one another's company, have good communication patterns (family members' listening to one another generates an important message of respect), show a commitment to each other (promoting each other's happiness and well-being), and cope with crises by uniting and supporting each other constructively.

In proposing strategies that focus on prevention of juvenile delinquency, one should view the early childhood years as an integral segment in a very complex process. Since children and families are influenced by interactions within the family and actions from outside the family, effective prevention strategies must be broad in scope and provide a broad spectrum of services that allow for developing a match between individual family needs and the appropriate services.

Continuity in human development must be emphasized. Continuity implies continuous nurturance for the child at each developmental level, with parents playing the key role and utilizing services from many disciplines, such as health, nutrition, education, and counseling. Not to be forgotten, however, is the need for the continuous development of the adults. People become parents at varying stages in their lives, a fact that affects their capability for assuming the parenting role. A parent may be a teenaged, unwed girl from a low-income family. The family may have little skill or few resources to provide emotional support, financial support, and adequate health care for her. Other parents may be mature adults, totally capable of assuming a parenting role and selecting from the traditional services, such as education and health, as needed for their child. However, even the most stable family may experience extreme stress, such as that caused by death, divorce, or extended illness, and may therefore need temporary outside support.

Many of the services needed by families are provided by existing community agencies. Two major problems exist, however. Many families who need assistance have limited skills in weaving through the often complex bureaucratic system. Second, and perhaps more important, an agency may offer only one service when the need is for multiservices. A case in point is the unwed, teenaged mother. She needs financial aid; she wants to complete high school in order to be more employable; and she needs child-care services. The three pieces in the puzzle need to match, but the coordination of efforts required may be more than this young mother can manage. She might have to contact five different agencies to complete the arrangements. She may contact only one and acquire financial assistance but still have no self-help skills or parenting skills, and the cycle begins again as the child grows through the years, modeling the mother's behavior.

In 1972, the Administration for Children, Youth and Families (ACYF) funded eleven national Head Start demonstration programs: the Child and Family Resource Programs (CFRP). The purpose of the CFRPs was to develop a number of models or approaches for integrating and coordinating programs that could be adapted by different communities to provide continuity in serving children during the major stages of their early development. The concept has merits all communities should consider. Linking community resources so that families have access to a variety of programs and services from a single center is both effective and efficient. Present economic trends suggest that programs to meet current needs will have to come from existing resources. Such a network in communities could minimize duplication of efforts and lead to an increase in available services. Linkages would also allow each agency or program to maintain autonomy, thus eliminating some of the turf-guarding associated with attempts to reorganize agencies more effectively.

Based on these views, it is proposed that communities consider developing Family Support Centers[8] as a means of nurturing the growth and development of children in a positive manner and as a means of enabling parents to maintain a key role in the family. If life experiences determine the motives that evolve into a particular life-style, then positive experiences in a child's life should enhance the opportunity for constructive goal setting and lessen the incidence of juvenile delinquency.

Appendix 8A
Family Support Center:
A Proposed Model

The Family Support Center should be viewed as a multifaceted operation. The scope of the center should include serving as a clearinghouse for inquiries; providing interface among agencies, institutions, and disciplines serving families and children; developing a network of agencies, organizations, institutions, and individuals serving children and families; seeking cooperation from employers in providing support to families; serving as a resource to the courts seeking assistance for offenders and monitoring any follow-up program; and adding to the knowledge base regarding social competence through program evaluation and research.

The goals of the Family Support Center should include the following:

Goal 1

To provide support and coordination related to the education of children, youth, and adults.

Related Services

1. Assist at-risk families in placing their children in programs such as Head Start.
2. Encourage churches and other service organizations to develop programs filling gaps in available services.
3. Develop linkages among programs such as Head Start and public schools that will facilitate continuity and a smooth transition for both child and family.
4. Arrange counseling, parent education, or home-based programs to aid parents in understanding the importance of positive child guidance, family health and nutrition, family communication, and family recreation.
5. Aid high-risk parents to learn how to provide care and stimulation for infants and toddlers.
6. Assist in developing a lending library for books, toys, and the like.
7. Develop linkages with programs offering educational opportunities for teenage parents that include completion of high school as well as the acquisition of good parenting skills.

8. Develop linkages with organizations offering educational opportunities other than traditional school programs for youth—for example, programs for the handicapped and for those who are not functioning effectively in traditional programs, such as children who would benefit from vocational programs.

Goal 2

To provide support and coordination related to health and nutritional needs of children, youth, and adults.

Related Services

1. Identify and develop a referral system for utilizing health-related agencies and funded health-care programs in assisting families in need.
2. Serve as a clearinghouse for disseminating health and nutrition information to parents, schools, day-care centers, and the like.
3. Develop referral and information services pertaining to life-support equipment or special equipment needed for handicapped persons.
4. Disseminate information regarding food assistance.

Goal 3

To provide preventive services to strengthen families.

Related Services

1. Serve as a clearinghouse to aid families in locating day-care services.
2. Aid in developing emergency short-term day-care services (that is, in the event of sudden illness of a parent).
3. Develop a "warm-line" telephone service that will aid families with nonemergency concerns that could lead to crises over a prolonged period of time (that is, support for the "new" parent).
4. Develop linkages with family-recreation facilities to promote opportunities for families to experience pleasant occasions together.
5. Aid in development of cooperatives for the purchase of food, clothing, and other household items.

Goal 4

To provide support and services to aid families in stress.

Related Services

1. Develop a hot line to aid families in emergency situations (that is, family violence).
2. Aid families in seeking legal assistance.
3. Develop a foster-care referral system that includes support service for foster caregivers.
4. Develop twenty-four-hour temporary emergency care for children (that is, for the temporary placement of an abused child).
5. Assist in the development of temporary shelters for families (that is, for safety following family violence).
6. Develop linkages to aid families experiencing alcohol or drug abuse within the family.
7. Aid families in developing linkages with support groups, such as Parents Anonymous or Alcoholics Anonymous.
8. Assist families in seeking emergency shelter, food, and clothing.

Goal 5

To provide legal information and advice.

Related Services

1. Develop linkages with representatives from the legal profession to assist families with legal matters.
2. Disseminate information regarding laws that have an effect on families and children.
3. Serve as a referral center for the courts and develop linkages between juvenile offenders and agencies providing remedial services.

This model is presented as a working plan to be modified, expanded, or adapted in the most effective manner to respond to the needs of an individual community. One must constantly ask, "What support system is best? For whom? Under what conditions?"

For the Family Support Center to be successful, long-term commitments are needed from those responsible for delivering services. The traditional American way is impulsive, often demanding immediate results. Attitudes that have become firmly rooted in a life-style, however, do not change immediately. Building a sense of trust takes time, yet parents can—by exercising patience and persistence—become an integral part of their child's life. We must move beyond stopgap measures to develop an intervention plan that focuses on the complexity and interrelationships of problems.

Notes

1. See D.P. Weikart, J.T. Bond, and J.T. McNeil, *The Ypsilanti Perry Preschool Project: Preschool Years and Longitudinal Results Through Fourth Grade* (Ypsilanti, Mich.: High/Scope Educational Research Foundation, 1978); and D.P. Weikart, A. Epstein, L.J. Schweinhart, and J.T. Bond, *The Ypsilanti Preschool Curriculum Demonstration Project: Preschool Years and Longitudinal Results* (Ypsilanti, Mich.: High/Scope Educational Research Foundation, 1978).

2. I. Lazar and R. Darlington, *Lasting Effects After Preschool* (Washington, D.C.: U.S. Department of Health, Education and Welfare, Publication Number 79-30178, 1978).

3. B.L. White and J.C. Watts, *Experience and Environment: Major Influences on the Development of the Young Child* (Englewood Cliffs, N.J.: Prentice-Hall, 1973); B. Bloom, *Stability and Change in Human Characteristics* (New York: Wiley, 1964); J. McV. Hunt, *Intelligence and Experience* (New York: Ronald Press, 1961).

4. U.S. Department of Health and Human Services, *The Status of Children, Youth, and Families* (Washington, D.C.: Department of Health and Human Services, Publication Number 80-30274, 1980).

5. Women's Bureau, *Report on Working Women* (Washington, D.C.: U.S. Department of Labor, 1980).

6. See U.S. Department of Health and Human Services, *supra,* note 4.

7. N. Stinnett, "Strengthening Families," *Family Perspective* (Winter 1979):3-9.

8. A model Family Support Center is proposed in appendix 8A, *infra.*

Commentary

Lawrence J. Schweinhart

One early-intervention program, the Perry Preschool Program,[1] was found to be related to a reduction in delinquent behavior, specifically self-reported delinquency of children at age fifteen. Our experimental group received an early-intervention program, while our control group received none. Before the intervention the two groups were very much alike, so that any difference between the groups appearing later can be traced back to the early-intervention program.

Children in the experimental group reported less delinquent behavior. In the control group, 15 percent reported taking property by force from another person, as compared with only 2 percent of the experimental group. The early-intervention program, in other words, reduced mugging from 15 percent to 2 percent.

In the category of "damaging institutional property," which could also be called vandalism, the program appears to have reduced the rate from 15 percent to 2 percent. Thus it appears that early intervention at ages three and four was able to reduce the rates of both of these activities ten and eleven years later.

How were we able to reach these conclusions? We selected children three and four years old, determined to be in poverty and at risk of school failure. They were judged to be in poverty based on the educational level of the parents, the employment level of the parents, and household density (that is, rooms per person in the household).

To determine academic risk, we used the Stanford-Binet Intelligence Test and, more particularly, the I.Q. range from 70 to 85, which was then regarded, correctly or incorrectly, as borderline retarded.

We then assigned the children to one of the two groups. The assignment process was important; the groups could not be allowed to differ on the basis of one having selected early intervention and the other not. The participants were totally without coercion with regard to participating; we decided whether or not they received the program. As indicated earlier, the resulting groups were extremely similar. The families were similar; the fathers' educational levels were alike, and the mothers' educational levels were alike in both groups. The maternal employment rate differed between the two groups when the children were three, but when the children reached age fifteen, we found the two groups the same, even in this respect.

We subjected the experimental group to an early-intervention program. At three and four years old, they attended a preschool program five mornings a week (twelve and one-half hours a week, two and one-half hours a day). Each week, the teacher visited the home of each child and discussed with the mother and child the education and development of the child. That program cost $3,000, in 1979 dollars, per child.

At age fourteen, the achievement level of the experimental group was 1.2 grades higher than the other group in reading, language, and arithmetic. Thirty-nine percent of the control group needed special education as compared with 19 percent in the experimental group. That particular finding is corroborated by the Consortium for Longitudinal Studies,[2] chaired by Irving Lazar. The consortium is a collection of twelve studies with essentially the same design. In six of the eight projects providing relevant data, the experimental-education program reduced the need for special education and/or retention in grade.

Shepard Kellam, at the University of Chicago, found that the aggressiveness of first-graders strongly predicted later delinquent activity.[3] I mention this to indicate that, in striving to prevent delinquency, we might be able to work within the educational system itself. Our program could have effects after ten, twelve, or more years, because the educational system is very much a tracking system, one in which the successful first-grader continues to be successful through whatever grade he completes. On the other hand, failures are found out quickly.

A researcher named Rist studied the behavior of teachers and children in inner-city classrooms.[4] On the eighth day of the kindergarten year, the teacher assigned kids to one of three tables. At table three, were kids who were poorer and kids who appeared to be less bright. At table one, were the kids that seemed bright and those of higher socioeconomic class. The teacher proceeded to talk to the kids at table one for the rest of the year, ignoring the kids at table three. Another example of tracking, which pervades the system, is assignment to special education.

It is not, however, just the system; part of the problem is the kids themselves. We found that the commitment to schooling was higher among kids who had attended preschool. Their motivation at ages six, seven, eight, and nine was rated higher. At age fifteen, they reported placing a higher value on school, doing more homework, thinking more frequently about going to college, and talking to their parents more often about school experiences. This early-education experience shifted the internal motivation of these kids. The children who had attended the preschool program were set up to interact with the school, to do better in school, to be recognized as doing better in school, and to receive the rewards from their teachers, parents, and peers. The action, therefore, is not just from the outside in or from the inside out; it goes both ways.

These scholastic findings were linked to a reduction in delinquent behavior—a reduction that did not just pop out of nowhere but resulted from the fact that the kids were doing better in school and were bound more closely to the scholastic-success framework.

With regard to economics—an important factor these days—the program cost $3,000 per year per child. If that money were never seen again, the program would represent a fine humanitarian one that perhaps cost too much. As it turned out, the benefits exceeded the cost. Because of the lower need for special education, the education of the average child in the experimental group cost $3,350 less. The projected earnings of the average child, because of the increased success in school, were $11,000 higher. Society realized, therefore, over $14,000 in benefits because of a $3,000 investment, or $6,000 in a two-year preschool program. In other words, these programs pay for themselves. Added to these benefits is the increased efficiency in the school system. With these programs available, schools can function better and more cheaply.

The relationship that we found between school failure and delinquency has a number of implications for other kinds of programs that might address scholastic failure. Such programs, as it turns out, may not only reduce scholastic failure but may carry the added benefit of a reduction in delinquent behavior.

Although this program will help, it will not cure. Many other public policies must be brought into place to deal with these problems. Conferences such as this one have a tendency to seize on some one thing as a solution; life is not like that. Multiple solutions to these problems are needed. This program seems to help. To suggest any greater importance would be a disservice.

On the other hand, as a result of the research in connection with the Perry Preschool Project and other projects, we can in fact advocate high-quality early-intervention programs that, despite a high initial cost, ultimately return the investment through benefits to society.

Moreover, it is not too risky to tie the kind of program we have talked about to the national early-intervention program, Project Head Start. Although there are differences between the programs that have been researched and the typical Head Start program, the similarities are sufficient to support the potential payoff of this early-intervention program and to warrant our endorsement of Project Head Start.

Another specific course of conduct would involve introducing state legislation providing for such programs. After all, it is at the state and local level that educational dollars—92 percent of them and rising—are spent. Since such programs can reduce the state's cost of education, investment in these kinds of programs is in the state legislature's best interest.

This, then, is the basic scientific evidence linking early intervention to reduction in juvenile delinquency. What we do with that evidence is up to all of us.

Notes

1. L.J. Schweinhart and D.P. Weikart, *The Effects of the Perry Preschool Program on Youths Through Age 15* (Monographs of the High/Scope Educational Research Foundation, no. 7, 1980).

2. Consortium for Longitudinal Studies, *Lasting Effects After Preschool* (Final Report of U.S. Department of Health, Education, and Welfare grant 90C-133) (Denver, Co.: Education Commission of the States, 1978).

3. S.G. Kellam, J.D. Branch, K.C. Agrawal, and M.E. Ensminger, *Mental Health and Going to School: The Woodlawn Program of Assessment, Early Intervention, and Evaluation* (Chicago: The University of Chicago, 1975).

4. R.C. Rist, "Student Social Class and Teacher Expectations: The Self-Fulfilling Prophecy in Ghetto Education," *Harvard Educational Review* (Reprint Series, no. 5, 1971), pp. 70-110.

Commentary

Hedda Sharapan

Fred Rogers, of "Mister Rogers' Neighborhood," was out of town and as he walked through the lobby of the hotel, a five-year-old boy looked up at him wide-eyed, and said, "Mr. Rogers, how did you get out of the box?" Fred Rogers carefully tried to explain to the child in a way he could understand how television works. The boy nodded his head through the whole explanation and finally asked, "Mr. Rogers, how are you going to get back into the box?"

That story is the basis for my remarks, because I see my role here as twofold: partly as a representative of "Mister Rogers' Neighborhood," which has been referred to by many professionals as a model for prevention, and also as a television producer. I will try in my comments to take the Mister Rogers philosophy "out of the box" to view the proposed model, and I will try to put the concerns we have raised in this conference "into the box."

Looking at Jan McCarthy's model from the "Mister Rogers' Neighborhood" perspective, I was struck by her strong recommendation that we focus across-the-board on all ages. I remember the letter that came to us from a woman of eighty-one who said, "I need to hear the message of 'You Are Special' just as much as the children do." People of all ages need that kind of help so they can, in turn, give care to others around them. Then, you are fostering a sense of community where people are interdependent rather than dependent on an agency.

Jan McCarthy's model also has a clear sense of the practical meaning of the word *support*. Coming from "Mister Rogers' Neighborhood," I understand how important that is for people.

In the *Philadelphia Inquirer*, reporter Susan Dundon recently told of walking into a friend's home while the "Mister Rogers' Neighborhood" program was on for the child in the home. The reporter, watching over the child's shoulder, found herself taking what she, as an adult, needed from the television set. She wrote:

> I envision Mr. Rogers having a slightly different show. He walks into his house, removes his jacket and his tie . . . he sings in that soft, magical voice of his, "I have always wanted to have a wife just like you . . . "

> And then he looks straight into the camera, straight into the eyes and says, "I bet you worked hard today. I wouldn't be surprised if you haven't had a minute to think about dinner. Did you know that empty casserole dishes are good things for pretending? Um-hm. They are. By pretending, just pretending, you can cook anything, a crab bisque, or a baked Alaska . . ."[1]

That is the sense of support that we have been talking about and that we all need so much. I hear in the model a tremendous amount of empathy for people who need to hear that warm voice that says, "I care about you." I like the emphasis on everyday human needs.

But I do have a concern: that the model is too extensive. It deals with three elements: intervention, prevention, and rehabilitation. We are so concerned about economics today. Where is the money going to come from? What if we have to choose among those three? The route that we would urge is the one we have taken on "Mister Rogers' Neighborhood"—that of prevention.

My last point with regard to the model concerns the sense of community. In developing models for communities, what size community do we mean? It brings me back to the word "neighborhood" from "Mister Rogers' Neighborhood." I think about the teenaged mother standing there with her crying child and saying to herself, "I am at my wit's end." First of all, when she finally does find within herself the strength to call for help, is she going to get on a bus (or perhaps three buses) and go downtown to find this support center? Or is it going to be a storefront place, easy to get to and involving people who are already trusted in her own community and in places that are important and personal to her?

Besides that physically close I-can-get-to place, a key element must be that warm, personal voice on the end of the phone saying, "I care." A great deal of emphasis must be placed in training those people who say the first "hello."

Let me now step into the role of the television producer and offer another component for the model. Can we use television for intervention and prevention and rehabilitation? Television is obviously much more than an entertainment medium. We at "Mister Rogers' Neighborhood" feel strongly about the positive socializing effects of television. One mother wrote us that she was about to abuse her child who had ripped out all the basting stitches that she had been sewing. The mother told us she was seeing red and about to pounce on the child. In that state, she felt she could have hurt him dreadfully. She then heard from her television the voice of Mr. Rogers sing, "What Do You Do with the Mad That You Feel?" She found in that voice the strength to gain her composure, went into the other room and counted to ten, and calmed herself.

When the program was over, she sat down and was able to talk to her son on his level. The caring voice of the "television neighbor" gave her a sense of support.

There is also research on the effectiveness of our programming. Stein and Friedrich[2] found that the children who watched "Mister Rogers' Neighborhood" for twenty minutes a day over a three-week period in a nursery school at Penn State increased in rule obedience, in task persistence, and in tolerance of delay. The differences were even greater for the children in the lower socioeconomic range. Television can be a source of positive support.

Do you know where I see the possibility of more positive television programming happening on a large scale? Through a system that has recently revolutionized our industry—cable television. It is a wide-open area for programming for the following reasons:

1. It has an enormous channel capacity, as high as 100 channels in major cities.
2. It brings a concept of narrow-casting, in which the economic base is the monthly fee from cable subscribers, and so there is a willingness to present programs for a small but committed audience.

Cable offers channels for specialized programming (news, women's issues, family movies, sports, children's material). Why not a twenty-four-hour-parenting channel that would be available by satellite to cable systems across the nation? Cable can offer the kind of education we have been talking about. Some of the possibilities are:

1. *Low-cost production of speeches or parenting classes.* For example, about two weeks ago, T. Berry Brazelton spoke in Rochester, Minnesota, and included in his talk were tapes of people interacting with an infant. One tape showed a parent warmly reacting to an infant. Another tape showed the infant reacting to a stranger, and a third showed the parent not reacting to the infant. Through that audiovisual experience, the audience learned to appreciate the kind of effect they have on their babies. People who heard Dr. Brazelton and watched his tapes said they went home wanting to hug their children and to spend time interacting with them. Why not offer that kind of audiovisual boost to parents through cable television?

2. *Two-way capability.* With a dual-wire system, cable can be more than a passive transmitter. People can communicate with each other. There can be an electronic visit between people in two different locations. In Reading, Pennsylvania, for example, senior citizens' in a nursing home are on one side of the screen with high-school students studying the Depression on the other. The students ask the senior citizens what it was like growing up in the Depression. Students thus learn the social, emotional, and political climates of that era from those who personally experienced it. But they are not only building an electronic bridge, they are building human relationships. I understand the teenagers go on to visit the people they have been speaking with on the two-way system. The electronic visit paves the way for the real visits.

3. *Request for a viewer.* Another remarkable possibility of cable is that a viewer can request that a particular tape be shown at a certain time. To the

parent who feels, "Right now I am at the end of my rope," there can be a program about calming and coping, maybe even five or ten minutes long. It can help parents feel they are not alone and that they can build on their own inner strengths.

Also, as with pretaped telephone messages, there can be cable-transmitted information available when parent's concerns are specific: for example, toilet training, bedtime fears, going to the hospital, starting school, and so forth.

4. *Local follow-up*. Another way to make the television connection more personal is to use the local social services. When we at "Mister Rogers' Neighborhood" produced a national parent program about divorce, we suggested that PBS stations have local outreach people available to answer phones afterwards, so viewers have a sense that help is available in their own communities.

5. *In-hospital patient education*. Cable also can program on a special channel that is fed to hospitals on an institutional link. At the conference, we talked at great length about the significance of the first days for mother-infant bonding. Many hospital patients spend most of their day watching television. Why not have special programs on what to expect with infants and with older siblings, on coping with some of the hard times, on ways to feel good about yourself, as well as on practical how-to knowledge? On the maternity wing, there is a captive audience. Young mothers tend to read every word of the booklets handed to them. They hunger for advice and, at the same time, need to feel they can trust their own instincts. Why can't their television viewing be meaningful in those two vital ways?

I am not suggesting television as an alternative to the parental-support center. Electronic connections through television must not be seen as a substitute for hand-on, personal connections. Further studies of Stein and Friedrich[3] reflected the need for people to enhance the television offering. When teachers used the material from "Mister Rogers' Neighborhood" and helped the children talk about it and play, the increase in those children's helping behavior was much greater than that of those who had merely viewed the same program.

Do not, therefore, look to television for the ultimate answer. It is a powerful medium, but it has limitations. I invite you to think of television as an ally. What is communicated, however, must be designed by people who really care. Caring is the deceptively simple basis of whatever models or strategies we plan.

Notes

1. S. Dundon, "Pretend, Just Pretend, That Mr. Rogers Is An Adult Friend," *Philadelphia Inquirer*, April 14, 1981.

2. L.K. Friedrich and A.H. Stein, *Aggressive and Prosocial Television Programs and the Natural Behavior of Pre-School Children* (Monographs of the Society for Research in Child Development, 1973, 38 [4, serial no. 151]).

3. L.K. Friedrich and A.H. Stein, "Prosocial Television and Young Children: The Effects of Verbal Labeling and Role Playing on Learning and Behavior," *Child Development* 46 (1975):27-38.

Roundtable

Lazar: Other studies have also been dramatic. The results of two such studies showed that a larger proportion of girls in the control group as opposed to the experimental group got pregnant while in high school. Among girls getting pregnant, almost all of those in the experimental group and almost none in the control group finished high school after giving birth.

All of these findings reflect a real shift in parental and individual values relating to learning. Preschool by itself, after all, will not do the job. There must be sufficient rewards for the parents as well as for the child if the heightened level of achievement is to last over the years. Preschool experience, however, sets it all in motion.

Schweinhart: We did no research on a compulsory program, although I think results would be different because the motivation of the parents would be different. Moreover, my guess is that the results would not apply to children in different situations from those in which our experimental group found itself. Under our model, one takes kids at risk of scholastic failure and addresses that issue; with children not at risk of scholastic failure, less improvement is likely. At least, that is what the research indicates.

Lazar: In one study, Palmer examined a subsample of middle-class kids in Harlem. That study suggested that, although such a program would not hurt such children, the major benefit is for children who are already behind the eight ball.

Stroud: If the program were given to everybody, would it not in effect push compulsory education back one level and accomplish nothing?

Lazar: What happens, in my opinion, is that Suzie comes home from nursery school doing things mother has never seen a three-year-old do before. The mother is enthusiastic about this, and at the same time Suzie likes what she is getting in nursery school more than what she gets from mother, sister, and brother. Now she demands the same kind of attention at home. A mutual shaping is set up. As the child does better, the mother gets more hopeful and more encouraging. There is mutual reinforcement, which is exactly what happens in a middle-class family.

In Chicago, there is an all-black school that for twelve years has been turning out National Merit scholars. These kids are essentially ordinary neighborhood kids, but they work in a highly motivated school situation under a spectacular teacher and person. The kids very quickly develop in such a school a sense that they can accomplish, and they *do*.

Scott: When these children get turned on to learning, they spend an inordinate amount of time reading and learning and do not have time for delinquency or other such activities. The principal demands performance and demands from the teachers that every child learn—pretty much on a timetable.

Lindgren: That is the flip side of the labeling process, a positive label.

Stoud: David Gilman said there is no American consensus with regard to good parenting. Does this mean no political consensus or no consensus among social scientists? Will trying to teach this result in a disaster?

Lazar: Sometimes it seems as if we are getting close to the radical ideas expressed in George Orwell's book, *1984*. Some baby books, however, like Dr. Spock's, have provided tremendous solace to new parents for many years. Now, with digital records providing an hour of television on a piece of plastic the size and thickness of a credit card, we will be able to have picture books.

Gilman: It is good that there are energetic people striving to better people's lives and, if some early childhood programs show promise, we do not want to douse them. Nonetheless, I recall the 1960s, when I did much welfare-rights litigation on behalf of poor people. My sole purpose was to secure money, and I was very successful. Because of my reputation, I could walk in with a welfare client and get $2,500 or $3,000 in special grants. Although I felt good about delivering the money, that welfare mother was back in my office a year later with the very same problem because there was no support system helping her beyond the money. The same thing happened with neighborhood health centers whose aim was to cure children of tuberculosis; ultimately, the children were sent back to the environment in which they contracted tuberculosis all over again.

What I am suggesting is support. I do not believe there are studies or data indicating that social services can get people out of poverty or that a little bit of money really helps. Support will be effective in altering life-styles only if issues such as jobs, housing, clothing, and essential services, which the public sector has not been able to deliver, are dealt with. We then need supportive services beyond those in order to change the way life goes on for people at the bottom. I think we oversell in believing that success in isolated instances can be replicated in vast numbers of people.

Lazar: We do need both micro and macro intervention simultaneously because each is necessary to the other's potential. With regard to school situations, however, we are no longer looking merely at isolated instances.

Scott: We must have a comprehensive family support system because almost all of these families have multiple problems. Few of them have one isolated problem to deal with. We now treat these problems in a very piecemeal way, sending people to twenty different agencies. If we merely rearranged the programs we have, we could actually improve the situation without inventing one new thing.

Audience Member: The record should reflect that a poll of the one-hundred most successful psychologist and sociologists in this country would result in a 90-percent agreement on the basic elements of good parenting.

Gilman: Such a poll should also ask the children of these experts whether they receive that good parenting.

Lazar: Perhaps as many as ten states have never taken advantage of the block grants for creation of a comprehensive integrated service system. It is now legally possible to put together such a system.

Scott: Dr. Steele mentioned some aspects of good parenting. The group study at Harvard suggests consistent discipline—not harsh, but consistent—affectionate, loving parents, and a positive model. These correlated highly with nondelinquency, regardless of other variables such as race, class, or the like.

Steele: The pediatrician can help by saying to the new mother, "I will see you in four or five days or call you on the phone and have you come into the office in two weeks," rather than saying, "I will see you in six weeks," which dismays the new mother. Such a helpful intervention requires no new federal grant but may completely change the mother's parenting ability.

Parents by and large want to do well and, if given some clues, will do well. Once the mother-infant interaction gets rolling, it will last a long time.

In our work with mothers and children, many of the children are often very depressed, very submissive, very quiet, very subdued, unable to be curious, unable to have pleasure, and so on. Under our preschooling influence, they begin to wake up and get active. Often, at first, the mother is horrified and feels her child is being spoiled; he is becoming an aggressive little monster instead of this nice, mild thing. But once we tide her over this, the discovery of the joy of an active, curious, developing, and growing child is extremely rewarding to her, and she, too, grows.

Bahlmann: One mother, whose children had been involved for about a year in our Big Brother-Big Sister Program, wrote us a letter indicating her appreciation of the help she and her family had received. Enclosed was a drawing of a little boy with his chin down in his hands and a caption that said, "I know I'm somebody because God don't make no junk."

9

Concluding Discussion

Identification of Children at Risk

Hollingsworth: The key is early intervention, and we need not wait for a judge to come in. It is a question of passive screening and identification rather than an adjudicated program. One important period for identification occurs, as Dr. Steele has said, in connection with the doctor's delivery of the child and during the primary six months. Screening at that time can spot physiological problems or other potential difficulties with the child. It is merely a matter of making that service available to the total population, and we already have the mechanisms to do that. But there is a totally different problem of identification after that initial period in the hospital and health-care setting.

Steele: Mandatory identification is a little bit misleading because it is more a question of using data already available and how it is used rather than mandating some new investigative procedure.

Surely we have data available from observing people during prenatal, clinical, and first hospital experiences and during early pediatric care. Other data, produced by preschool or by other teachers, are available at the time the child is in kindergarten or first or second grade.

Lazar: Parents have not generally challenged competent professional diagnosis. The challenges that have led to restrictive laws have resulted from the employment by school districts of incompetent people who put labels on kids. Indeed, a competent professional will include the parents from the beginning and will not reach a diagnosis without talking to them.

Schweinhart: Two different kinds of criteria can be used to determine whether a child receives intervention. The Head Start type of criterion is the income level of parents. The handicapped-legislation approach focuses on specific characteristics of the child. Most of our discussion has focused on the individual child, but a number of times the notion of focusing on groups rather than individuals has been mentioned. Translated, that means focusing on characteristics of families in terms of income rather than characteristics of individuals. We could stress providing early childhood intervention to children from families who have been statistically placed at risk because of the nature of the resources available to them. That approach perhaps avoids a lot of problems that have been mentioned.

Stroud: No matter which of the two is used, a person put into a program compulsorily will challenge the program on the basis of his constitutional rights. We should use voluntary programs.

Lazar: In eastern Kentucky about fifteen years ago, we set up a program affording reliable, broad-based, and helpful data about the period between initial gestation and birth of the child, on the one hand, and his entrance at the age of five into the compulsory-education arena. We and the Departments of Health, Mental Health, and Social Welfare trained a group of paraprofessionals to do, among other things, intake on the spot. Every newborn was visited within five days of arriving home or of being born (if born at home). The paraprofessional was generally someone living nearby who brought information to the mother, assessed the family situation, and invited the mother to a weekly coffee meeting with other mothers. If the paraprofessional saw a situation requiring professional intervention, she could radio from her car one of seven public-health nurses who would come by that very day.

The public-health nurse would deliver a service or would arrange for an appointment at or admission to a nearby clinic the nurse was associated with. Multiprofessionally staffed, the clinic was a medical, psychiatric, and educational one, with a nursery school and a program for the handicapped—all in one location. If necessary, the nurse could admit directly into a regional hospital.

If the initial visit required no such action but involved only the gathering and dispensing of information, a follow-up visit was made three weeks later, then every month until the child was six months old, and then every other month until he was eighteen months old. This process built up such rapport that the mother felt comfortable asking this familiar person, who was an access to resources, for help when it was needed, whether that help was medical aid or a sewing machine.

The women's meetings, run by social workers, were essentially mutual exchanges of information and a general introduction to educational materials. The family was thus connected into a system allowing help if needed (even in isolated settings) but with no intrusion since the person did not have to invite the helper into the home. There was, I might add, no requirement that the people go to such meetings or that they use any of the services. But they loved the help and used it.

Bahlmann: What happens when the money runs out?

Lazar: Money for Appalachia is different; it is there if needed. The problem of continuation involved not money but rather a new set of cabinet officers who were so turf-conscious that they could not accept the idea that a person not on their payroll would do admissions to their program. Turf protection is the largest problem in coordination efforts.

Stroud: I should point out that collecting data can create problems. For example, collecting data from newborn babies and comparing those receiving one kind of treatment with others can be called "human experimentation" and be subject to regulation.

Also, if teachers are required to create identification data, parents will have access to those records and, if unhappy with them, can challenge them. This can result in a big fight or even litigation.

Chinlund: In connection with Dr. Lazar's Kentucky program, perhaps Dr. Steele could elaborate on what one trains paraprofessionals to observe in the postnatal days, since this could be important for identification of the model.

Steele: A nurse on the ward, for example, can observe how a mother feeds her baby: Does she seem interested in the baby, or does she put the baby on her lap, shove a nipple into its mouth, and look casually around the room? If the nurse concludes that the mother does not know how to take care of a baby adequately and needs some help, she can go to the mother and say, "We can help you to learn how this works better so your baby is fed better." That, rather than being intrusive, is just what a beloved grandmother would do. On the other hand, if the nurse goes to the mother and calls her incompetent there is trouble.

Chinlund: Are records of the observations kept?

Steele: The chart would note, "Mother is having difficulty feeding her baby; learning how to use a bottle."

Chinlund: If help were rejected, would that be indicated?

Steele: Yes. Indeed, rejection of help indicates an even higher risk. But help is almost never rejected.

McCarthy: Pediatricians helped organize such a program in my community. First, they examine the child to see if there are health problems. They also assess the mother's ability to interact. They do a follow-up for all babies born in the hospital by sending a visiting nurse to the home within five days after the child has gone home. There are some data gathered about home conditions; for example, that the mother is unwed and from a very low-income family, or that the home seems so unkept that health problems for the child might result.

Mothers are invited to participate in the program and most do. The local mental-health center maintains an outreach program that makes regular visits to these mothers, and a lot of data on the children has been gathered.

Stroud: If we do not deal with those who reject the program, will we not miss those who are most at risk?

Steele: To some extent, that is a problem. It requires doing more outreach and finding a way around any problem. If that is done, most people will respond. A permanent rejection is almost unknown.

Lazar: In their longitudinal studies, Larry Schweinhart and other investigators approached over 2,000 patients—not to offer them service—but (ten years after the service) to come into their homes for an hour or more in order to interview the children, secure school records, and the like. Only twelve refused. So we are indeed talking about an extremely small percentage. Even an abusive parent rarely turns down an offer of help.

No human service in the United States is offered in sufficient quantity to meet demand. No community has enough human services. There are not enough doctors in Rochester, Minnesota, not enough day-care centers in Connecticut, and not enough psychiatrists in Beverly Hills, California. Why talk about compulsion, therefore, when we cannot meet the need, in any event?

Stroud: The most interesting programs mentioned here—for example those discussed by Dr. Steele, Mr. Lazar, and Mr. Chinlund—are all designed to do something other than prevent delinquency. That very strong attribute of those programs makes it much easier to get around the prediction problem, which has a tendency to inject an ideological component in some areas. A program designed solely to identify predictors of delinquency, intervene, and change people in some way will get the most rejection from people and create the most legal problems with regard to things like compulsion. This is not to suggest "fudging" on the issue, but a family-service center and its delivery of parenting information can be justified by goals other than reduction of delinquency. The question for us, then, is whether reduction of delinquency should remain an explicit goal or whether we should give up on that.

Methodology and Scope of Remedial and
Preventive Programs

Lazar: We begin with the fact that any government service is intervention. We distinguish between those considered important to the public safety and welfare, which we make compulsory, and voluntary ones. The state of the art does not yet justify compulsory services in the behavioral-sciences area. We have no evidence that compulsory counseling is effective. You cannot tell people to help themselves. We should quickly review past efforts to integrate services and look at a new model that seems to have made some headway. Every participant in the conference is a human-service worker and would not have been there if there were any question about the validity of some kind of intervention.

Chinlund: Compulsory counseling is a more complicated matter that involves more than a judge telling Johnny he must get counseling once a week until he is a good boy. Lately, there have been attempts to require Johnny to go to one or two sessions just to see what is available. That is what happened in the Morris Model of the prison. The compulsory beginning unhooks the person to a certain extent from peer pressure. From then on, however, he goes voluntarily. This system is therefore a mix of voluntary and compulsory.

Lazar: It should be pointed out that a macro model need not be nationwide or, indeed, even statewide; it could operate at the community level or any level larger than the individual.

Conrad: For example, Indiana could have a universal state service for young people without any other state doing it. It is, of course, very unlikely.

McCarthy: There are eleven Child and Family Resource Programs (CFRPs) presently existing. These CFRPs are very similar to the family-support-center model outlined in my chapter. These eleven were funded in 1973 by the Administration for Children, Youth and Family.

Lazar: These programs, in existence for about seven years now, have been fairly well received. The Louisville program, the Human Services Coordinational Alliances, started not as a program but as a service to agencies. Anyone seeking any service from a private or public social agency in Louisville fills out a sheet asking eighteen basic questions. The sheet goes into a scanner right there in the agency, and a computer reads out on line a list of those agencies in that person's zipcode area that have such services available and for which the person is eligible. The services are identified not by their professional labels but through a very clever series of questions that begin with goals.

On a regular basis, the central organization supplies to every agency the size and characteristics of their caseload and uses the same data to assess shortages in the community. Agencies are also told what other agencies their clients are using. This makes collaboration among agencies more likely and more effective. For example, one agency might outstation one of its people at another agency that deals with a common client, and the client may be spared one or more separate trips. Through this device, a team is assembled, but every agency retains its own identity. No one is coordinated out of existence. This process has led to greater and greater integration of agency goals around clients and families rather than around case labels.

Bahlmann: Is there a diagnostic component?

Lazar: The agency doing a formal intake may do a diagnostic test.

Bahlmann: What elements should our model have?

McCarthy: One component should be the independence of the community. We must not think in terms of one giant center serving the world. A community center that provides easy access—a tangible center to which people can relate—is crucial. These would be neighborhood centers.

Hopson: Apart from the services to be delivered by this agency, what is its legal and political structure?

McCarthy: My model leaves that open for involved professionals to decide.

Lazar: One agency structure already exists. Federal law mandates the creation of information and referral centers, I and R centers. The federal government will provide 90 percent of the cost. The I and R centers, however, do not provide the services themselves.

Chinlund: The model calls for more than I and R centers. Indeed, beyond those listed, particularly under "goal one," items of a more specifically service nature—such as courses in parenting or in communication or other support for family life—would be provided by the center. The I and R centers, on the other hand, seem to provide only referral.

McCarthy: We do not wish to create an agency to do things, like family counseling, already being done by others. The center would bring people together.

Chinlund: Very few places really are providing services such as family counseling. There are people ready to refer but not enough ready to say, "We'll do it." I would hope that our center would say, "We are not the only ones that may be able to do it, obviously, but this is one of the things that would happen here." This place must be attractive to people. If a court is telling people to go to an awful place that nobody would want to go to, the whole question of compulsion jumps up. The compulsory dimension will not be important if the person wants to go anyway.

Lazar: Section two of the document [McCarthy paper] calls for the integration of all services except legal services. Those are separate. Over the past thirty years, the problem has been that people making proposals are willing to coordinate everybody else but themselves. There is no reason for a separate arm. Part three, therefore, should be integrated with part two.

Conrad: Must the document use the phrase "at-risk family"?

Stroud: I would delete it. Without it, there is one set of problems and with it, another.

Lazar: When Dr. Steele and his group see a new parent in the nursery exhibiting the initial charactersitics—for example, failure to make eye contact with the baby—no one says to the parents, "Your child is at risk of abuse." They say, when the parent goes home, "The nurse will come by next week." Labeling is not necessary. If places are not labeled "delinquency-prevention centers," they might even work. In Minnesota, the program was sold to the legislature as a local parent-education program that would help parents do a better job with their kids.

Schweinhart: Let me provide some counterpoint. We must be careful not to develop an elaborate program to do something already being done less formally. We must not be locked into a centralized approach that might not provide the best use of available resources.

Steele: A famous atomic physicist once said that for every truth there is an equal and opposite truth. We are in the dawning of a new effort and, even if we cannot specify precisely its result, let us try to do some good for the human race.

Schweinhart: Let me distinguish between two types of thinking. In one case, we are talking about a pretty clear set of postulates linking the lack of early childhood intervention to scholastic failure and scholastic failure, in turn, to delinquency. If we follow through on the same series of postulates in this [McCarthy paper] more comprehensive approach, the linkages would be a lot weaker. The postulate in the more comprehensive approach, as I see it, is, "Do good things for people, and the world will get better."

The notion of looking at scholastic failure instead of delinquency is very valuable, but it should not cause one to say that we are dealing with delinquency here but will not talk about it; we will just talk about doing good things for people. The power of that logic is much less.

Furthermore, many of the proposals listed in the document are good ideas that are therefore difficult to challenge. But we have no evidence, to my knowlege, that established state and local networks for the delivery of services, for example, will prevent delinquency.

Hopson: Perhaps I am alone, but I am not comfortable with a recommendation for a multipurpose family referral center of undefined size, shape, and description. That is not the best way to use whatever dollars are available, especially since it adds still another level of social-support services at the top. If I could figure out a way to get the legal system to engage pediatricians into the social-service model in terms of home visits with the nurses and into a rather elaborate at-risk registry with child-care and state departments of health, then there is a chance. But that is another issue.

Lazar: If we are to put our money into a single service, the best would be a well-developed child-care, early-education program. But that is something much more expensive than what the Welfare Department will pay for in day care and must include basic nutrition, education, and other components.

Conrad: We must develop something between a micro and macro model with regard to day-care nurseries or day-care centers, properly monitored and staffed, that offer the services working mothers require. That need is now urgent and will become more so as the decade goes on.

Such nurseries or centers should be built into any kind of program. They are essential for gathering information and for providing maternal health training. Even upper-middle-class mothers like cooperative-day nurseries, from which they get many services, including maternal training. If such are effective where mothers can pay for them, they should be available for people who cannot pay for them and for whom they are still more urgent.

Schweinhart: The kinds of results I talked about earlier involve the investment of $3,000 per child. Although that may sound expensive, programs that are considerably cheaper will probably hurt rather than help kids.

Lazar: Indeed, there are data supporting that. There is no question that we probably hurt kids and waste money if we do not do it right.

McCarthy: The problem is that we have often tried to do things as cheaply as possible. As a result, the money has been lost.

Stroud: Once one moves from the experimental into the routine delivery of some kind of service or intervention, must it not be capable of administration by ordinary government employees? Ms. Sharapan's and Mr. Chinlund's presentations, for example, relied heavily on the love and caring of the deliverers. I do not think you can get that on a routine basis by government employees.

Hopson: We can do better in that regard than you think.

Lazar: West Berlin, which already has a universal day-care system, is putting into place a universal infant-care system. The personnel are chosen according to their capacity to show love, and not according to their degrees, courses, or experience. Those in charge are looking for certain kinds of personalities and will work with those picked.

Stroud: Will that happen in Indianapolis, Louisville, and other cities?

Lazar: If the decision is a local-level one and, if we did not get talked out of it, we could make it happen.

Chinlund: One can use the Carl Rogers list, the very well-established Rogerian List, instead of the taboo word "love." Although it sounds better, the Rogerian List still means love.

Stroud: But are there not the same complaints about our current welfare system—that the staff are not caring, do not love us, try to cut corners, and become company people? Will not the same thing happen when the new program gets established on a large basis?

Bahlmann: That is because of the way we structured the welfare system. We have turned Welfare Department personnel into money changers and report filers, as opposed to individual care workers. With appropriate control and focus on what one wishes to accomplish, a caring organization can be maintained.

Lazar: The structure we created for the welfare system leads it to exist not for clients but for the county commissioners. But there are concerned people who know about these things, and, after all, love is not that complicated.

Hollingsworth: Love is very complicated. Human-service love is extremely complicated and may not last long because purposes and expectations are not well defined. The "Mr. Rogers" people do a very good job; however, without their structure and purpose, they would not have a message to broadcast. Love in human-service work is extremely complicated, and teaching it is even more difficult.

Lazar: I am not trying to teach it; I am trying to select for it.

Webster: I attended the conference because it promised to focus on the connection between intervening early in the lives of children and preventing juvenile delinquency. Now I hear the discussion focusing on providing good things generally, which might have an incidental effect on juvenile delinquency. I want to know what we can do to reduce juvenile delinquency.

Lazar: Delinquency is not an illness. As I stated earlier, delinquency is not a characteristic of an individual, but of a situation. We know the correlates of that situation. We know the conditions under which that set of symptoms flourishes more than any other. If we can reduce the set of pressures that produces those combinations, we are preventing delinquency. But delinquency is not the only thing that that set of pressures can produce. I have never tried to tell anyone that I will eliminate delinquency. I cannot sell that.

McCarthy: If the stated purpose of the center is to prevent delinquency, many people may not want to use its services, and the center will not get people very freely. We want to reach the upper-middle-class family suffering from severe drug abuse or alcohol problems that threaten to destroy the family just as much as we want some of the low-income people. The center should be viewed as a positive support base for anyone in the community.

In our state, day-care centers are still licensed by the State Department of Public Welfare. As a result, people still say, "I don't want to send my child to a Welfare program." A stigma is attached that deters people from seeking certain services of a preventive nature. We must recognize this problem, or we will kill the center before it is opened.

Bahlmann: That phenomenon is reflected in the fact that a significant number of children on welfare rolls are not adopted because they are welfare kids.

Foust: I am sold on your approach, but how do we make it marketable for others? Certain listed conditions tend to place children at risk of delinquency. The bullet that will best hit the most of these conditions is increasing family support in all respects, and the way to do that is to set up family and child support centers with a flexible range of resources, most of them referral, but including some needed services for which no referral is possible.

Conrad: The prevention of delinquency is an incidental benefit of this program. Although the program probably will result in prevention of delinquency, it will not eliminate delinquency, and the program should not be evaluated on the basis of a reduction in delinquency. It should be justified and evaluated according to whether it is delivering services that people in the community need and that will facilitate happier childhoods and happier families.

Bahlmann: A member of our audience said earlier that basic delinquency is an attempt to meet basic needs that cannot be met in constructive ways. What we are all saying is that we would like to give persons a constructive vehicle for meeting these needs so they need not resort to nonconstructive methods of meeting them.

Conrad: Many people in cities such as Indianapolis, San Francisco, and elsewhere have legitimate needs that are not being met but that could be.

Chinlund: I have an added concern. We know that a combination of strengthening families and strengthening schools will help kids avoid the road toward delinquency. There are blueprints for doing that (for example, *Schools Without Failure*, by William Glasser, and *Peoplemaking*, by Virginia Satir). If a commitment to an Indiana adaptation of *Schools Without Failure*[1] and to an Indiana adaptation of *Peoplemaking*[2] resulted from this conference and were elements of a model to which the Indiana Lawyers Commission commits itself, we would have taken a tremendous step forward. The already mature state of the art would be advanced. This is not "fuzzy thinking" but an approach that is working and helping communities across America, and this tremendous step forward would mean changed lives for Indiana kids.

Hopson: What bothers me is that this model is the kind of model drafted some forty years ago when family-service associations were set up. Those were designed to coordinate and deliver services. Then United Ways were created; after that, came coordinating agencies that are support groups for United Way. For about four decades, then, we have been hearing about this kind of information and referral system of coordination. In the next ten years, delivery of social services will be hard pressed for funds and resources, and, therefore, we get nowhere by talking about building another grandiose model for coordinating and for making referrals. That would just result in another social agency that, to the extent that it is good, will have some power in the community but will have the same turf problems and the like. If we have some identifiable way to reach certain kinds of kids with rather specific types of services through the educational system or early identification of at-risk babies, we have something to focus on. The idea of creating another coordinating agency, however, leaves me cold.

Steele: The model has some content different from that of previous coordinating agencies.

McCarthy: If the coordinating agency is too much involved in providing services, it ends up competing with the people it is trying to coordinate, thus causing difficulty in implementing the program. What must be emphasized is that when a family needs a service agency, it usually needs more than one service and must deal with five or six different agencies, often without the needed skills. People who go to the Welfare Office only to be sent to four other places to get forms signed become discouraged and give up. Most of the things people need are already in operation somewhere in the community. We need a way get the whole thing together.

Hopson: Will this model, like the old-fashioned neighborhood center, put all the service-delivery units in one building, or is it an information and referral system?

McCarthy: It is a combination.

Lazar: It is a combination that would utilize services already there, supplement them, and, if necessary, fill in the gaps.

McCarthy: It would also bring in groups to fill the gaps. There are people wanting to fill some of these gaps who do not know how to go about it. With regard to family counseling, for example, three or four groups here in Indianapolis have asked me about getting together to provide family counseling because they have been doing it but without much of a clientele.

Lazar: We have many curious structural problems, some of them legal. The record-keeping requirements of individual funding agencies tend to keep services apart. Frequently, the reporting systems are incompatible.

A family has a set of problems as a cluster, but we have no way of treating the people as a family. We break the family down, with the people fitting on some lines but not on others, and with one service that will not be much help unless another service is also provided. This program presumably would provide a single-entry intake system allowing one to utilize whatever is out there in the community. The model may not be neat, but it is feasible, whereas the old-fashioned, central community center is no longer feasible in this country.

Expectations and Strategy

Chinlund: What was exciting about this meeting was discussing doing something that has not, as far as I know, been done before. If the proposed program is a network of support centers providing for a significant group of people an understanding of communication and of family life and the like, an emerging, maturing art at present, this program will be the basis for subsequent enlargement. If the services are good and are provided to a broad base of people, and if, according to whatever little tax money may be available, a quota of people could be assigned by school counselors or judges in numbers that would not swamp the program, the program would provide a very exciting model calling, perhaps, for extension.

Webster: Even if we have a consensus for a model that, providing needed services, will incidentally reduce juvenile delinquency, how do we present whatever we come up with to the public? Whether one is trying to sell a program to the legislature, or to a community-service center not involving funding by the legislature or the Congress, people's concerns must be addressed.

Lazar: It can be done. But there must be a commitment with regard to what you want to do and how far you want to go with it. There must also be recognition that labels are important, can make or break programs, and can lead us down blind paths. A program specifically to prevent delinquency would take us down a blind path.

A good example is the suicide-prevention center, which may cause the suicide rate to go up. On the other hand, in Louisville, it was discovered that suicide was concentrated in certain census tracts of the city. Rather than say, "We are going to march into that neighborhood and prevent suicide," specific support services, and family-support services in general, were increased. Incidence of suicide has gone down for three consecutive years.

In Hartford, Connecticut, in building a referral system that the whole community would use, they relabeled the Welfare Department machinery the Community Life Society. They remodeled the offices to look like insurance offices. The whole population began to use the services.

Schweinhart: The Head Start program, funded at the level of about $850 million, is another illustration that early childhood programs can be sold. The research on childhood intervention discussed earlier received much publicity in December 1980 just as the Carter Administration was formulating its budget. Significantly, when the Reagan Administration took over, it—reflecting interest in research documentation of this approach—

bought the same assumptions and endorsed an increase of $130 million dollars in its budget. Head Start is probably the only nonentitlement social program receiving an increase in the Reagan budget. That testifies to the power of this logic in the political arena.

Lazar: A good CFRP program is easier to sell than Head Start. Once we list the necessary services and support their establishment, we need not say they should be delivered in the same way or by the same agency in all places. We could, however, suggest a mechanism that might be used to organize the delivery of those services. If we do not specify the minimum services required, many political and turf problems will result.

I do not know of a single other community using the early-identification process now employed in some hospitals in Denver, although it is not hard to teach.

Bahlmann: Dr. Hollingsworth, how do we identify the at-risk group?

Hollingsworth: We do know that children with social, emotional, physical, and maturational lags do not do well in school and are at a higher risk of being somewhat delinquent later on. We also know that there are about 7 million kids in special education at the kindergarten, first-grade, and second-grade levels. Consequently, we know there is a large number of kids with specific characteristics suggesting high risk.

Bahlmann: Should the population be expanded beyond those groups? As indicated earlier, we do not want a sign on the front door stating that this is the targeted group.

Lazar: Another approach to this, which almost became law last year, is currently called the Child Health Assurance Program (CHAP).

Bahlmann: In Japan, all children are routinely seen about eight times during their first year and a half of life for comprehensive physical, social, and psychological examinations that are not, incidentally, initially administered by physicians, but by trained nonphysicians. The object is to identify children at risk for all sorts of problems. Some people in this country, however, were upset about implementing a similar program here, and consequently, CHAP did not succeed here.

Foust: Having dealt for the last eight years with some of the problems associated with creating new programs and services, I have become sensitized to the idea of turf. If the newspaper were to report tomorrow that our group had recommended family-support centers, some existing agencies would immediately respond that they were doing this very thing. It may be a matter of terminology, but perhaps our orientation is slightly different from theirs. If our program is oriented a bit more toward child and family, the turf problem might not be so acute.

Anderson: I agree. One significant difference in the structural model is a support center—a very necessary component—that is a point of dissemination much more broadly based than in some other programs. The program actually focuses on the family and is intended to develop a system of support services providing help when needed to the family in the most effective way. We have discussed nurturing, love, guidance—all the things so important for individual growth. The program puts responsibility where it is most effective. If it cannot be done there, then the family-support center or others might do the job, but the focus is much different from that of other coordinating components in the past.

Foust: The structure should be left loose since we do not know what might develop. But, to begin with, we need a more specific orientation toward children and child-delinquency problems.

Stroud: Providing needed services, but with a loose linkage to delinquency, presents two problems. First, the criterion for success will be difficult to specify, whereas with a tight linkage model, the success criterion can be specified fairly well.

Second, the loose linkage route is more likely to raise an ideological component, therefore making the proposed legislation a lightning rod for political dispute. For example, you can more easily sell a program designed specifically to reduce delinquency, especially when money can be saved within the same administrative agency. Such a program gets the attention of the legislature.

On the other hand, a proposal to teach people how to be parents will scare the legislature because there is no consensus with regard to that. Fundamentalists and the Christian school teachers do not even want fire regulations applied to their systems nor do they favor child-abuse laws. This is not, incidentally, because they want to beat their children but rather because they are worried about state intrusion into the family's rearing of their children. A program to teach parenting could not be sold in twenty years.

Lazar: It may not sell in Indiana, but it has already sold in eight states and will spread within the next two years since block grants will make it easier to implement.

Bahlmann: Obviously, a model that is ready to be implemented will have the best odds of securing block-grant money.

Hopson: Should one put his money into this model and make Dr. Steele's hospital personnel refer the noneye-contact parent to it, which, in turn, will provide the visiting nurse? Or does one put the money into Dr. Steele's program to hire extra nurses who, working out of Dr. Steele's hospital, visit the family?

Bahlmann: That is not the choice. At this point, Dr. Steele's program will still exist. If parent "X" comes into the model program needing such help, a screening mechanism will send the parent to Dr. Steele's program. The model program is not providing the service.

McCarthy: Exactly. Dr. Steele has a good ongoing program. We might even get him involved with other people and expand it. In our community, we had one fine pediatrician doing this, and some of us asked him to share his information. Now we have six pediatricians doing some of the things Dr. Steele has talked about. But someone had to be able to coordinate it.

The model might provide the center that could capitalize on his services by making them known and by involving a lot of people in the community in it. Although there are good things going on in the community, sometimes people two blocks down the street are not aware of them. The center's constant job would be to seek out information and know what is going on in the community.

Lazar: Dean Hopson's question reminds one of the endless debate that pits family day care against center day care. What we must do is determine the minimal things that ought to be available and then, for a given community, devise the best way of putting them together. What is already there, what is not already there, who will pay, what needs to be filled in, and what is the best governance situation for that community? The difficulty with a uniform model for all communities is that not all communities are uniform.

Steele: A purpose to minimize the wastage of childhood and youth through school failure and delinquency by supporting family development, for example, will be much more acceptable and will not require us to prove too much. We can improve school performance and general developmental matters. Our purpose is to identify problems as early as possible in the child's life so that the family can get remedial measures as early as possible.

Hopson: We must set out the mechanisms for that early identification so that the appropriate children can be identified, followed, and treated. If the politics of the fall of 1980 taught us anything, it is that a general statement calling for the doing of good for all people will not, with regard to funding, be accepted for the next ten or fifteen years. Head Start gets funded because of the publicity describing it as a service that could produce results. We cannot talk about general social-service programs to make people better or life more enjoyable. Society might fund a program identifying early childhood problems and strengthening early childhood development, a program that will pay dividends later on.

Chinlund: I disagree. Funding for the strengthening of the American family is possible. Somebody sponsors that Johnny Cash sign saying, "Is there a family in the house?" If this group of experts says what it wants to do, and that it really means business, funding could be secured.

Hopson: Your definition of strengthening families is not that of the president of the United States.

Chinlund: There is enough common ground.

Hopson: To some, strengthening the family means going back to the rod, as indicated when a child-abuse reporting statute causes 3,000 people to protest the law on the grounds that "sparing the rod and spoiling the child" is prohibited.

McCarthy: The phrase "at-risk" means something different to each of us. Some would view it from the perspective of child abuse, others from the perspective of children with special needs, and still others from different perspectives. Although perhaps confusing, the phrase is intended to be open and flexible. After all, there are many reasons for which a child may be at risk. We need a system for using the facilities, the expertise, and the services that are in the community.

Schweinhart: It is important to focus on what the federal government has been funding. In terms of child versus family criteria, diagnosis versus income, if you will, the number of children zero to five years of age served by programs for the handicapped in 1979 was about 15,000. The number of children served through a variety of federal programs under income criteria was 1.6 million. Therefore, one thousand times as many children are served without any official diagnosis of a specific risk. In short, many more children are being served because they belong to a group at risk or in need.

Bahlmann: One point being made is that the government, by setting up these criteria, spends money on people not in need. This leads into the "truly poor" debate.

The second point is that the federal government is trying to put control back in the local community so that the local community, given the money, will set the criteria. I think state block grants will result in fewer criteria and less money. Under the state-block-grant system, however, there will be the ability to sell an effective program to the local control process. We will now have fewer federal conditions attached to the money, but the local community will be more accountable.

Lazar: It is difficult to argue in favor of using only one set of criteria; this means providing services to one group that needs them versus another such group. A larger problem and a central conflict involves the worth of human life as opposed to private property. Fancy diagnoses can waste a lot of money. In fact, the kids in the most trouble make themselves known rapidly.

Bahlmann: Our discussion so far indicates the need for a document with a preamble specifying purpose along the lines referred to by Dr. Steele, and a body describing the client, the linkage, and a model structure. If such a document can be put together, our duty will be to comment on it and ascertain whether there is a consensus with regard to the model. Obviously, any compulsion involved in the structure must be within accepted legal principles.

Lazar: Two recent documents that might be valuable sources are the statement of the Colorado Governor's Office on the goals for Colorado youth and that of the North Carolina Governor's Office on children and families. Both are very thoughtful.

Conrad: Other states have done the same thing. To be sure, we need not appease persons with a very narrow, ideological position. But we must be sensitive to the current and broadly based concern in the country about excessive governmental intrusion into families.

Steele: The wording of the document is crucial. It might be wiser to refer to, "Early recognition of problems in need of help," rather than, "Early identification of children at risk."

Anderson: This group is contributing to the beginning of a whole new era and approach, one that prevailed before we quit being responsible for what happens to our families and our children. Now, that responsibility is being pushed back on us, and this group, as experts, can provide a model for dissemination to other states to assist them in their own development with enough flexibility to accommodate all components. Love cannot come from Washington, D.C., to the heart of the person one is trying to help. It must be done one-to-one. As William T. Sharp has said, the question is not precisely one of equality, but rather of individualized equality, since we must take the individual as he is and with what he needs in order to be equal.

William T. Sharp: As a member of the Indiana Lawyers Commission, I want to thank the participants for sharing their very considerable wisdom in this very free-flowing presentation. They have not sown seed on barren soil. Since the Indiana Lawyers Commission is a lawyer's organization, what we have learned will make its mark on this state through the various organizations in which members of the commission participate.

Notes

1. W. Glasser, *Schools Without Failure*, 1st ed. (New York: Harper & Row, 1969).

2. V. Satir, *Peoplemaking* (Palo Alto, Calif.: Science and Behavior Books, 1972).

10 Summary and Consensus

Delinquency should be viewed as a characteristic of a situation not of an individual, and such a characteristic is subject to a changing community. Reducing pressures and conditions known to further delinquency is a worthy objective. Since delinquency is an attempt to meet basic needs in unconstructive ways, a system that meets such needs in a legitimate way is needed.

Because a preschool child does not receive the developmental attention that is later received in school, it is easy to underestimate the great importance of the first four years in the child's life. These are critical years in the development of social skills and roots of intelligence, and at no later time will the child develop or learn as rapidly. This is not to suggest that early intervention must be limited to those four years, but rather to emphasize that they are critical ones in a child's development. Moreover, as so well stated by Jan McCarthy, "Families are the primary socializing agent of the child and it is essential that the parents remain the most important adult figures in the child's life . . . "

Assuming for the time being that child development can go awry in very early years, one is immediately confronted with the problem of identification of children who are at risk of maldevelopment and later delinquency. The consensus is overwhelming that early intervention for the at-risk child is justified. The real question is probably "how" rather than "whether," but that meeting of the minds still does not solve the problem of identification. A consensus, not quite so overwhelming, appeared that mandatory identification is not really required. For example, the data base for discovery of maldevelopment or "risk" is available by at least the second grade of school; indeed, prior to that, deviant tendencies surface in day care and preschool.

There are two ways to identify children at risk: one is by the individual identification just mentioned, and a second is by some criterion other than individual—a criterion associated with risk of delinquency, such as low family income, poor school performance, child abuse, single parent, and the like.

Substantial information is available to identify populations at risk. Although identification by criterion will produce some false positives, it avoids many of the problems created by a program for individual identification. Stated another way, identification becomes less important if there is a macro approach, since the services will be supplied to everyone in a certain category. If the program adopts a micro approach—that is, treats individuals with certain characteristics that place them at risk—identification becomes a larger item.

Many times, individual identification occurs as a routine matter while other services are being provided. For example, within a few days after a child is born, notes on the mother-child relationship will have been made at the hospital. In the notes, there may be indicators that the mother-child relationship or parenting is in trouble. Thus, an at-risk child is individually identified at a very early time.

Nevertheless, even with the facility of the macro model, it is not certain that all the available data will be used because of privacy problems or because parents may succeed in restricting their use. This privacy problem would seem to require further exploration, particularly with regard to its legal implications.

It is probably true that the kids in most trouble rapidly make themselves known. That truism would suggest that a developed program of early intervention need not limit itself to a macro approach but could also make provision for inclusion of those troubled kids who at some point (in preschool, for example) have made themselves known. The consensus then was to develop a macro model for broad-based identification, but loosely so that individually discovered children at risk could be helped.

It also is valid to suggest that identification need not be exhaustive. On the one hand, complete examination of every child to identify risk is not only probably impossible but also so expensive that it becomes impractical. On the other hand, so much good can be done by helping those who are identified either through macro grouping or through individual identification during participation in another program that acceptance of oversights would seem to be the better course to follow, at least initially. As one participant said, "[I]f it is a general service offered to all in a certain category, the fact that it strengthens the already strong, reinforces the adequate and saves the weak from chaos is probably all for the good." One caveat: Whatever means of identifcation are used, at all costs one should avoid a label of "predelinquency" or similar nomenclature that tends to stigmatize the child.

For further discussion we shall assume that the problem of identification has been at least satisfactorily solved and that we can move on to the problems raised by intervention itself. (Indeed, even the wisdom of the term *intervention* may be in question. Perhaps a better term would not have any connotation of the book, *1984*.)

Brandt Steele succinctly stated the purpose of intervention: "to minimize the wastage of childhood and youth through school failure and delinquency." Seeing the strengthening of families as a logical first step, he stresses the necessity for identifying problems as early as possible in the child's life and reinforcing the family's resources by early remedial measures.

Again, one must ask whether only a consensual intervention should be the approach or whether it is necessary to employ a nonconsensual, involuntary methodology. The first conclusion was to "intervene by all means." As to the nature of the intervention, the consensus seemed to be to avoid involuntary intervention even though the identification may have been involuntary. About the strongest position taken on involuntary intervention was that compulsion to get contact might be justified, but there should be no compulsion to continuance—for two reasons. First, compulsion itself raises legal, ethical, and public-acceptance problems that might be insurmountable, and second, compulsion simply does not work. Ken Stroud makes the point that, although it rarely occurs, parental rejection of help for the child indicates that the child is at the highest risk and will not be helped unless a compulsory model is used. The answer to that seemed to be that parental rejection is rare enough that an occasional rejection does not justify encountering the problems incident to a compulsory model of family extension; we are not going to meet 100 percent of the need in any event.

One good way to stay out of the compulsory-services trap with its attendant legal questions, it has been said, is to make delinquency prevention a dividend of another family-support program (for example, parenting). Furthermore, the program should not be justified on the basis of preventing delinquency but of providing a service. The weakness of that is that generally doing fine things for people reduces the linkage to delinquency, whatever value that linkage has. The choice seems to be between maintaining good programs to improve the family and maintaining specific programs to prevent delinquency, on which choice the group seemed to be fairly well split. Nevertheless, the consensus favored early intervention for children at risk through a consensual/voluntary model. This model should be maintained except where public safety is jeopardized or violations of law have occurred, in which cases compulsion may be warranted.

Likewise, there was agreement that a model should be developed that could be widely replicated. With that apparently decided, the next problem concerns the kind of remediation program to be developed.

All agreed that the model should be one of family-support services: family extension. There was less agreement on specific details. For example, some asked whether the group was trying to duplicate family-service or comprehensive mental-health clinics or community-service centers. Many respondents seemed to be saying "No," but a specific explanation of the difference was lacking.

The family-support center could be simply a referral center. For example, the social-security act provides for information and referral family-service centers in which 90 percent of the cost is maintained by the federal government. Such a center does not provide services. Conference opinion, however, was probably unanimous that an effective family-support center must offer some basic services, lest clientele be frustrated by being directed from place to place. Whatever program emerges should define the minimal level of services available for each community and provide the coordination and organization skills necessary to begin operations. Each community could then do resource inventories, feasibility studies, governance structure determination, public-relations studies, and the like. As the need becomes obvious, additional specialized services can be added.

What are the components of an appropriate model? Beyond the macro approach, whom should it serve and under what conditions? The participants agreed that the model should serve all children and families at risk (that is, be nonexclusive), although staffing, adequacy of resources, and the sheer complexity of the problems present serious difficulties. Where practical, appropriate agencies should share resources and coordinate efforts, although so-called turf problems may develop. Any model should include the following elements: identification, screening, diagnosis, research, information, parenting training, provision of services, referral when the service is not provided for in the model, outreach, day care, training, a network of local-state services, and evaluation. The model center should be easily accessible to the community and foster a strong positive relationship with it. A generally accepted suggestion was that Glasser's *School Without Failure* and Satir's *Peoplemaking* be blueprints for the model. It is important to remove as much of the bureaucratic flavor as possible. All staff should have the capacity to nurture with sensitivity and love. (The Berlin Infant Care System is an example of such a model.)

Contributors concur that sufficient information and research now exist for the development of a plan. Emphasis should now be on implementation. Marketing and political strategies must be developed to assist in obtaining the approvals necessary to establish the system.

About the Contributors

Barbara J. Anderson is assistant director, Child Mental Health, for the Indiana Department of Mental Health, Indianapolis, Ind.

David Bahlmann, the conference moderator, is executive vice-president of Big Brothers/Big Sisters of America, Philadelphia, Pa.

Stephen Chinlund is chairman of the New York Corrections Commission, Albany, N.Y.

John P. Conrad is senior program officer for the American Justice Institute in Sacramento, Calif.

Cleon H. Foust is executive director of the Indiana Lawyers Commission, Indianapolis, Ind.

David Gilman is executive director of the New York State Temporary Commission to Recodify the Family Court Act, New York, N.Y.

David K. Hollingsworth is an instructor at the University of North Carolina School of Medicine, Chapel Hill, N.C.

Dan Hopson is dean of the School of Law, Southern Illinois University, Carbondale, Ill.

Mary Hughes is director of Public Health Education for the National Foundation of March of Dimes, White Plains, N.Y.

Irving Lazar is professor and chairman of the Department of Human Services, New York State College of Human Ecology at Cornell University, Ithaca, N.Y.

Jay Lindgren is executive officer, Juvenile Releases, for the Minnesota Department of Corrections, Saint Paul, Minn.

Jan McCarthy is coordinator of the Early Childhood Educational Program at Indiana State University, Terre Haute, Ind.

John Monahan is professor of law, psychology, and legal medicine in the School of Law at the University of Virginia, Charlottesville, Va.

Richard O. Ristine is vice-president of the Lilly Endowment, Inc., Indianapolis, Ind.

Lawrence J. Schweinhart is codirector of the Center for the Study of Public Policies for Young Children, High/Scope Educational Research Foundation, Ypsilanti, Mich.

Joseph Scott is professor of sociology and anthropology at the University of Notre Dame, Notre Dame, Ind.

Hedda Sharapan is associate producer of "Mister Rogers' Neighborhood," Pittsburgh, Pa.

Brandt F. Steele, M.D., is professor of psychology at the University of Colorado Medical Center, Denver, Colo.

Kenneth M. Stroud is a professor at the Indiana University School of Law, Indianapolis, Ind.

About the Editors

Fernand N. Dutile is professor of law at the University of Notre Dame. He received the A.B. from Assumption College and the J.D. from the Notre Dame Law School. After service with the U.S. Department of Justice in Washington, D.C., and on the law faculty at the Catholic University of America, he returned to Notre Dame in 1971. He is a member of the Maine Bar.

Cleon H. Foust received the J.D. from the University of Arizona College of Law. Mr. Foust spent several years both in private practice and as deputy attorney general and attorney general of Indiana. His career has been principally academic; he spent twenty-nine years at the Indiana University School of Law, Indianapolis, where he taught criminal law.

After serving as dean of the law school from 1967 to 1973, he joined the Indiana Lawyers Commission, Inc. The lawyers commission, a subsidiary of the Indiana State Bar Association, engages in criminal-justice projects and programs. Currently, Mr. Foust is professor emeritus at the law school and executive director of the lawyers commission.

D. Robert Webster, senior attorney for the Cummins Engine Company in Columbus, Indiana, received the A.B. from Indiana University and the J.D. from Harvard University Law School. A member of the Indiana Bar and the American Bar Association, he has served in private practice, on the faculty of Indiana Central University, and as director of research for the Indiana Lawyers Commission.